American Catholic Laity in a Changing Church

William V. D'Antonio
James D. Davidson
Dean R. Hoge
Ruth A. Wallace

Sheed & Ward

Sheed & Ward™ is a service of National Catholic Reporter Publishing Company, Inc.

Library of Congress Catalog Card Number: 88-60114

ISBN: 1-55612-247-0

Published by: Sheed & Ward
115 E. Armour Blvd. P.O. Box 419492
Kansas City, MO 64141

To order, call: (800) 333-7373

Contents

Preface

This book is about how American Catholics are continuing to respond to the social, political and demographic changes of the 1960s, 1970s and 1980s. The period under study extends from the pre-Vatican II era of Pope Pius XII to the present papacy of Pope John Paul II. The data for this book come from our 1987 survey of a representative sample of the American Catholic laity, 18 years of age and older.

American Catholics now in their adult years began their lives in a Church in which the laity's prime role was to kneel, "pray, pay and obey." Now they live in a period when more and more of the laity find that role unsatisfactory. Thus, our 1987 survey probes the degree to which Catholics have changed their image of themselves and of their roles in the Church. It also explores their changing perception of the moral and teaching authority of the Church and its leaders. That is, the survey focus is on who they think should have the moral authority to decide whether actions like using contraceptives are sinful or not, and whether the laity should have the right to participate in Church decision-making that affects their lives.

This book had its origins in informal discussions between William D'Antonio, Executive Officer of the American Sociological Association and a member of the Board of Directors of the *National Catholic Reporter* (NCR), and the paper's editor and publisher, Tom Fox and Bill McSweeney. The discussions focused on the upcoming Synod of Bishops in the fall of 1987 to examine the role of the laity in the Church. The Synod was to take place just after the second visit of Pope John Paul II to the United States.

Fox and McSweeney saw the value of a nationwide survey that would provide the U.S. bishops with information that could help them in their synodal deliberations. D'Antonio agreed to carry out a survey if he would be given full authority over its design. Fox and McSweeney agreed, with the understanding that they would be invited to comment on the survey and offer suggestions during the several stages of pre-testing. They also contributed $20,000 to help cover the cost of running the survey. And it was agreed that NCR would have first use of the data for a major story, after which the team of sociologists working with D'Antonio would be free to use the data for their own scholarly purposes. An additional grant of $5,000 was received by the team from Fr. Andrew M. Greeley, and those two grants proved sufficient to carry out the study and data analysis. The authors wish to express their deep appreciation to Tom Fox, Bill McSweeney and Andrew M. Greeley for their financial and intellectual support of this project.

D'Antonio invited Drs. Ruth Wallace, Dean Hoge and James Davidson to join him in the project.

William V. D'Antonio served as Executive Secretary of the Society for the Scientific Study of Religion from 1970-76, and then as its president. He has been publishing recently on the changing relationship between families and religions, including a book and several articles.

James Davidson, Professor of Sociology at Purdue University, is interested in the relationship between religion and social/economic justice. His research has focused on why some affluent churches are more successful nurturing faith and promoting social justice than others are. In a recent book (*Mobilizing Social Movement Organizations*), he showed how local congregations can form ecumenical coalitions and increase their impact on issues related to the causes and consequences of poverty.

Dean Hoge, Professor of Sociology at the Catholic University of America, has published extensively in the sociology of religion, with books focused on aspects of change and continuity in the Catholic Church. His most recent book, *Future of Catholic Leadership*, won a first place award under the category of professional books at the 1988 gathering of the Catholic Press Association meeting in Boston. A committed Presbyterian, Hoge has shown himself to be a sensitive chronicler of Roman Catholicism in America.

Ruth Wallace, who brings an important female perspective to the project, is a Professor of Sociology at George Washington University. A former member of the California Sisters of the Immaculate Heart, she is a Past President of the Association for the Sociology of Religion and a long time member of the Society for the Scientific Study of Religion. She has co-authored a book on gender roles, published articles on women in the Church, and has been writing of late on feminism and sociological theory.

The study took shape over numerous meetings, and three pretests carried out in several parts of the U.S. The Gallup Organization was hired to carry out the national survey, which it did during April and May of 1987. Gallup conducted 20-minute telephone interviews using the system of random digit dialing, with 803 completed interviews of Catholics in non-institutionalized settings, aged 18 and over. The Interview Form appears in the Appendix.

Our study focuses on questions of individual freedom, personal autonomy, moral authority, and democratic versus autocratic decision-making in the Roman Catholic Church in the last years of the 20th century. In this book we elaborate the results of the findings originally reported in the *National Catholic Reporter*, September 11, 1987, place them in historical context, and reflect on some of their more salient implications.

In addition to the invaluable support provided by Fox, McSweeney and Greeley, the authors wish to acknowledge the contributions of Drs. Teresa Sullivan and Mary Ann Lamanna of the Universities of Texas and Nebraska Sociology Departments respectively. They not only commented on the questionnaire in its pretest form, but also participated in the discussion of the findings held at Catholic University in July, 1987.

The authors wish to thank the following persons for their critical reading of the manuscript: Charles Davis, Mary Anna Colwell, Mary Ann Lamanna, and Bill McSweeney. Many of their suggestions have been incorporated into the body of the report. And their editorial efforts are hereby gratefully acknowledged. Of course, the authors alone are responsible for the data presented, the analysis and the implications that have been drawn therefrom.

While we consider this book a group effort, and share responsibility for the project, each author volunteered to write two chapters, which were revised several times after editorial comments from the others. Thus, D'Antonio was primarily responsible for Chapters 1 and 3, Hoge for 4 and 7, Davidson for 2 and 8, and Wallace for 5 and 6. The concluding chapter was a joint effort.

1.

Laity and Leaders: A Changing Relationship

"It has often seemed that for Catholics obedience is the only virtue just as the sin of the flesh is the only vice." French Theologian Yves Congar offered that apt comment on the Roman Catholic Church during the turbulent years of Vatican II and *Humanae Vitae*. And for those of us who had been brought up in the pre-Vatican II Church, that statement did sum up the Church's teaching. It was as simple as that.The point was that Roman Catholics were part of an autocratic, hierarchically structured religious organization which expected unquestioning obedience from its adherents.

But "pray, pay, and obey" no longer characterizes most Roman Catholics in the United States, and this fact is a major reason for carrying out our study. As our data will show, an increasing number of Catholics believe that they should make their own decisions in moral matters based on empirical information, even when the latter may challenge traditional values and beliefs. Expanding education over the past thirty years has fostered growing dissent from many traditional teachings of the Vatican.

Our study documents the areas and the extent of this dissent among the laity. It also reveals the degree to which the laity believe they have a right to participate in the decision-making life of the church.

The Heritage of Individualism and Autonomy

American culture, nurtured by Protestantism and small-town democracy, has profoundly influenced Catholics in this nation. Among the many observations made by Alexis de Tocqueville during his tour of America in the 1830s, two are important to our study. Tocqueville, in his classic *Democracy in America,* remarked on the strong tendency toward personal autonomy among the then predominantly Protestant population. This character trait also included a sense of social obligation that led citizens to develop voluntary associations to overcome social and political problems at local, state and national levels. Americans not only valued freedom for themselves as individuals but insisted on the right to organize themselves into associations that owed allegiance to no higher authority, religious or political. These two features of individual and social life have provided an important cultural base to U.S. society.

Tocqueville observed how personal autonomy, so strongly fostered by Protestantism and the English heritage, was also restrained by it. By personal autonomy Tocqueville meant that the "citizen of the United States is taught from infancy to rely upon his own exertions, in order to resist the evils and the difficulties of life; he looks upon the social authority with an eye of mistrust and anxiety, and he claims its assistance only when he is unable to do without it . . ." (Tocqueville,1984: 95).

This atmosphere created an individualism that encouraged people to think matters through for themselves. Society fostered the growth of individual consciences that were to be free of external constraints, civil, political or religious. In the religious sphere, the Protestant churches instilled among the faithful a strong belief that they were responsible for their own salvation. But Tocqueville observed that this same kind of self-orientation, in the political and economic spheres of life, could lead to a society that would tolerate a self-interest which ignores the common good.

For Tocqueville the key to avoiding the worst consequences of this kind of individualism lay in the way the leaders had structured the polity. That is, the right to participate in every aspect of community life led the people to a gradual awareness of their mutual dependence. Over time, they came to appreciate "the close tie which unites private to general interest." (p. 196). Thus, added Tocqueville, "the free institutions which the inhabitants of the United States possess, and the political rights of which they make so much use, remind every citizen, and in a thousand ways, that he lives in society. They every instant impress upon his mind the notion that it is the duty, as well as the interest, of men to make themselves useful to their fellow-creatures . . ." (p. 197) Thus, political participation could be expected to remind each American of the common good.

Tocqueville was reflecting on the question: How is it that we are both individual and social at the same time? What is the relationship between the rights of the individual and the individual's responsibility to help insure the common good? And, further, what are the consequences, for ourselves as individuals and for the groups of which we are part, of the way we see and think of ourselves as individuals, and act as members of social groups? Not only do people see themselves differently, but the norms or rules guiding their behavior vary according to a variety of factors such as the racial, ethnic, religious, and class characteristics that mark them in a pluralistic society.

Tocqueville provided us an acute insight into the ways that American Protestantism helped frame the relationship between the individual and the social. We need to understand that relationship as we examine how Roman Catholics are gradually changing their own understanding of the relation between the individual and society.

The ancestors of American Catholics who came to the United States from Germany, France, Ireland, Poland, and Italy found themselves in a society whose basic values about freedom and autonomy were new to them. Thus, even as they were slowly acculturating to the ways of American society, they were being warned from the Vatican that such values were a central evil of the modern society. As we shall see in the coming pages, the struggle between personal autonomy and obedience to central authority is a major feature of the current crisis in U.S. Catholicism.

Assimilation to American society could not be avoided. Despite the warnings and the efforts of the Vatican to counter the effects of the American emphasis on autonomy and voluntary associations, American Catholics became increasingly influenced by the ways of American society. While, out of deference to Rome, they were slow to join any of the Masonic Lodges, they proceeded to join other associations. There was no shortage of other associations to choose from, ranging from bowling leagues to garden clubs, to national civic-social organizations, political parties and labor unions. And, of course, there were organizations like the Knights of Columbus, Altar Societies and Holy Name Societies, that had some of the features of voluntary associations, but which were tied to the Church and ultimately submissive to it in matters of faith and morals. And gradually there appeared the independent associations like *Commonweal* and the Catholic Worker Movement led by Dorothy Day.

The place of voluntary associations in the life of American society was aptly described by Daniel Bell (*Life*, 1967):

It is the extended network of voluntary associations which has been the source of so much independent initiative, in politics and social life, in the United States. One might argue that with our increasing urbanization such civic consciousness would diminish and that in this decline one could find the source of the dis-orientation that individuals feel in the large, urban environment. And yet I would argue to the contrary. In American life today there is probably more voluntary association, more local community and suburban newspapers and more participation in a variety of organizations, professional, hobby and civic, than at any previous period in American history.

To an important degree, Catholic laity are just now approaching the level of autonomy and voluntary associational activity concerned with but independent of Church authority that has been the hallmark of Protestants for two centuries. The growth of personal autonomy and of voluntary associations with a Catholic religious orientation is very much a product of the socio-political ambience of American society, not of any Church-sponsored movement. On the contrary, the hierarchical Church's prime concern has always been obedience to its official teachings, and control over organizations having any relationship with Catholicism. Church leaders have been reluctant to acknowledge from the pulpit the primacy of the informed conscience, insisting that the correctly informed conscience would necessarily be in conformity with Vatican teachings.

Neither did the Church encourage the growth of voluntary associations with a Catholic orientation, whether it was a journal of opinion like *Commonweal,* or the laity-led Christian Family Movement. For the nature of voluntary associations is that they are subject to no authority outside of themselves. Thus, even though many organizations like the Knights of Columbus and religious orders have some of the characteristics of voluntary associations, they are ultimately subject to Rome. The Jesuits were reminded of this in the early 1980s, as were the several orders of nuns in the conflict over the signing of the *New York Times* newspaper ad in 1984. (In this regard, the decision of Barbara Ferraro and Patricia Hussey to leave the Order of the Sisters of Notre Dame de Namur suggests that the Vatican can still wield power sufficient to gain its immediate objective even when a religious order tries to stand its ground.)

In some ways even more telling has been the widespread opposition of Church leaders to autonomous labor unions in Church-related hospitals, cemeteries, parochial schools and colleges. This opposition flies in the face of the encyclicals on the rights of workers to organize into free labor unions in civic society. Apparently, it is one thing to cheer for Solidarity in Poland, but another to welcome it within an official Catholic Church-sponsored organization.

Since the 1960s Catholic voluntary associations have flourished in America. Ruether (1987:72) observed that "Almost all of the most lively expressions of American Catholicism come from new initiatives, developed either by religious orders or by laity, which operate autonomously or quasi-autonomously from the hierarchy but nevertheless function as expressions of the Catholic community. One has only to think of the Catholic Worker Movement; the Catholic colleges, increasingly governed by lay boards; the independent Catholic press led by the *National Catholic Reporter;* the network of Peace and Justice centers; the networks of Catholic women, both religious and lay, such as the National Association of Religious Women and Chicago Catholic Women; Catholic advocacy groups of various kinds, such as Dignity, Catholics for a Free Choice and the Association for the Rights of Catholics in the Church, not to mention the Chicago Call to Action."

Nor are these evidences of autonomy only the work of progressives. For example, the Right to Life Movement began under lay leadership independent of the hierarchy. The right wing also has its own independent publications like the *Wanderer,* and *Faith and Reason.*

The growth of these associations provides dramatic evidence of the Americanization of traditional Catholic forms. The new forms may be just as vital as the old, but they are different. And they have come into maturity in the last 30 years. It is hard to believe that it was in the 1950s that Mons. John Tracy Ellis and Thomas O'Dea had raised serious questions about the vibrancy of Catholic intellectual life in the United States (Ellis, 1956; O'Dea, 1958).

Research on American Catholics before Vatican II

While Ellis and O'Dea lamented the lack of contributions to American intellectual life by Catholics, empirical research was probing the question in several related ways. The tension between obedience and autonomy, for example, was revealed in the way the early parish studies carried out by Fichter (1973) were suppressed, lending support to the critics who claimed that the Catholic commitment to obedience stultified its intellectual life.

The tension was revealed in another way in Lenski's classic study of religion in American life (1963). He surveyed Catholics and Protestants in the Detroit area in 1958. On a number of important behavioral, value and attitudinal characteristics, he found Catholics in the Detroit area to be sharply distinguished from Protestants and Jews. As expected, Catholics had higher fertility rates, lower divorce rates, more focus on family, less interest in voluntary associations, much higher church attendance, and lower achievement aspirations.

Among the questions Lenski asked in his study is one that touched on core societal values. It read : "If you had to choose, which thing on this list would you pick as the most important for a child to learn to prepare for life?" It then asked the respondents to rank order five value options:

1. to obey

2. to be well liked or popular

3. to think for himself

4. to work hard

5. to help others when they need help

Jews and Protestants were much more likely than Catholics to choose intellectual autonomy (thinking for oneself); Catholics more often chose obedience. It was not that Catholics rejected personal autonomy; but they were more likely to see obedience as the primary value.

Lenski related this finding directly to vertical mobility; those who valued autonomy were more likely to be vertically mobile in the society, since it apparently made for more achievement orientation in school and in work. In terms of income and occupational attainment, the data supported the hypothesis. The emphasis on personal autonomy was a key finding for Lenski, for he also saw personal autonomy as a vital element in defense of American democracy. It fostered respect for freedom and support for voluntary associations. Rightly understood, such autonomy meant thoughtful, reasoned participation in the life of the community.

A reliance on obedience, on the other hand, would correlate with restraints on individual freedom, as well as on one's capacity to be competitive in school and in the world of work.

Lenski was focusing on a central dilemma of Roman Catholic life at a time when many Catholics were still first and second generation ethnics, still tied closely to ethnic churches, still more commonly in blue collar than in white collar occupations, and still less likely to finish high school and college than Protestants and Jews. In 1958 there was no reason to think the Church would not be the same a decade later. But neither Lenski nor anyone else was prepared for the changes that would follow the death of Pope Pius XII and the ascendancy of Pope John XXIII.

Vatican II and the Process of Change

John XXIII may only be a historical note for young people in 1988, but he is much more than that for Catholics over age 45. When he succeeded Pope Pius XII in 1958, it was assumed that he would be only an interim caretaker pope. But he soon startled the Church with his announcement that it was time for a second Vatican Council, time to open the windows of the Church and let some fresh air in. And, he added, we should all pay attention "to the signs of the times." Well, from then until now the winds have been blowing strong and show no sign of letting up. Nor has it been possible, yet, for those who are opposed to some or all of the results of Vatican II to close all the windows. Let us review some of the changes that have come to the Roman Catholic Church in the past 25 years.

The extent of pluralism, that is, diversity of beliefs and practices, that marks the Roman Catholic Church in the United States today has impressed every serious observer and worried many. Before Vatican II, the Church appeared to many as a monolith in its religious beliefs and practices. However accurate that image was then, it does not fit the Church of the 1980s. In some ways, the Church today looks something like American Protestantism, with several denominations. Just as Glock and Stark (1965) placed the various Protestant denominations on a continuum, so we can suggest that the Roman Catholic Church and its adherents in the United States form something of a continuum of religious types, from the most traditional (like the Protestant fundamentalists), to the most progressive (like the United Church of Christ).

Other people would have us compare contemporary Catholicism with Judaism, with its orthodox, conservative, and reform groupings. The image is helpful as it allows the reader to see that a range of religious beliefs and values may be held by a people who still have some overriding identification. Hoge (1987:43) sees pluralism as an inevitable result of the assimilation process:

> Assimilation, in my opinion, should not be seen as either good or bad from a Christian ethics viewpoint. The New Testament severed Christianity from an identification with a particular culture ("There is neither Jew nor Greek," Gal. 3:28), thus de-emphasizing assimilation questions. Yet in the real world people have strong feelings about assimilation versus maintenance of tradition, with predictable outcomes. An experience of assimilation produces parties in the group undergoing the process, which battle each

other over the specifics of assimilation—such as the use of one language or the other in worship, specific laws of ritual or purity, religious versus secular education, intermarriage with outsiders, and so on. Parties of this type have arisen in Americn Catholicism as well as in other immigrant religious groups.

Autonomy and associational activity, as key ingredients of American democracy, have greatly influenced the American Catholic population during the past 150 years. In the present context, the question is, "What are the proper limits on individual conscience and free association within the Roman Catholic Church?"

The limits have been expanded or contracted in recent years by the different leadership styles of Popes John XXIII, Paul VI and John Paul II.They are expanded when the Pope stresses collegiality and joint participation in decision-making (as with John XXIII in establishing Vatican II), and contracted when the pope dissents from or ignores such joint participation and goes his own way (as with Paul VI in his dissent from the majority decision of the Birth Control Commission which he himself had formed). Thus, since Vatican II we have been witness to the increased tension between the newer pluralistic tendencies and the traditional hierarchical, authoritarian structure; between rational discourse built on the value of personal autonomy and group decision-making, and a form of rational discourse that is anchored in obedience built on the claim to tradition.

Pluralism Within the Church

Several events reflect the growth of pluralism and democratic tendencies in the Catholic Church during and since Vatican II:

1. At the time of the Vatican Council there were waiting in the wings theologians like John Courtney Murray, Yves Congar, Hans Küng and other scholars, plus bishops and cardinals with ideas that would change the structure of the Church and the daily lives of its adherents. It is in-

teresting that despite the Church's highly authoritarian, hierarchical structure prior to Vatican II, there seemed to be no shortage of theologians, philosophers, canon lawyers and others ready and able to point the Church in the direction of a more collegial, democratic, rational modern organization once the Council was underway. This says something about stereotypes of monoliths; it also says much about the impact of western democratic societies upon Catholic thinkers.

2. The bishops at Vatican II created their own dynamic beyond the confines of any original agenda. They reflected their own socio-cultural environments, and for the first time they found themselves in lengthy dialogues with colleagues from other parts of the world. And they learned how to stand up to the Curia.

3. John F. Kennedy was elected President of the United States in 1960, providing a lesson for Catholics and others. Kennedy, educated at the Choate School and then Harvard University, was at best a marginal Catholic in any traditional sense, but his social ideas came out of the American Catholic tradition that marked so many other Democratic leaders of the 20th century. While Kennedy was identified as a Catholic, and used his Catholic identity with political astuteness, he believed that reason and not ideology were the hallmarks of his time, and that people of good will could sit down and work things out. But more than anything else his election laid to rest the fears of many people that a Catholic president would not be free of ties to the Vatican.

4. Student, Civil Rights, anti-war and Women's movements that spread during the 1960s and 1970s, stressed the use of reason and personal rights as well as social rights and responsibilities. Catholics were caught up in these movements as were others, and almost all of the movements challenged traditional authority in one form or another. For example, the student movement challenged the authority of university administrations to act *in loco parentis* in regulating social conduct.

5. The growth of an educated Catholic population in the United States facilitated the rationalization process. Data reported by Greeley (1985:

31) show that Catholics in the 1980s have not only increased their rate of college attendance, but they are now found in large numbers among those who have earned graduate degrees. As the proportion of Catholics who are college-educated, upwardly mobile and suburban approaches the rest of the population, their attitudes and values have become increasingly similar to the rest of the middle class. And perhaps just as important, the large majority of Catholics (Hoge, 1987: Ch. 1) do not go to Catholic colleges.

6. The documents of Vatican II provided new conceptions of the laity in the Church and new ideas of collegiality in the relationship of the bishops with the pope, opening the way for a restructuring of the Church as organization.

7. *Humanae Vitae,* on the other hand, was an attempt to restore traditional theological thinking. A birth-control debate has raged within the Church since the establishment of the Birth Control Commission by Paul VI in 1963 (Hoyt, 1968). Today there continue to be numerous study groups of Catholics engaged in serious discourse about questions of parenthood, sexuality, and family planning in an urbanizing world. One theologian who participated in the Notre Dame Conferences on Population and Family Life during the 1960s stated the matter simply when he said: "You know, we never really looked into these issues before; we just accepted the teachings."

The birth control debate was waged in the mass media as well as within the Vatican walls, and it proved to be a heady experience for Roman Catholics. Greeley (1985: 216-217) explains it this way: "Because of the Council, the establishment of the Birth Control Commission, the expectation of change in the Church and the changing values of the clergy, by the early 1970s, almost nine-tenths of American Catholics did not think birth control was a sin at all."

8. Other events of Vatican II also helped foster pluralism.

Vatican II changed the laws on fast and abstinence. Meatless Fridays were no longer mandatory for Catholics; instead Catholics were encouraged to take personal responsibility for choosing a penance as a symbolic gesture in remembrance of Christ's death. It was not a case of eliminating the practice of doing penance. Rather than having the institution choose the type and time of penance, the individual Catholic was encouraged to decide for herself or himself on the form of penance to be self-imposed. It was now to be an exercise in personal autonomy.

In addition, this new norm regarding fasting also opened the door to independent thinking for the Catholic believer. The fact that eating meat on Friday was no longer considered a mortal sin raised for many Catholics the larger question about the attribution of sinfulness to other actions. It had, for many Catholics, a kind of "hole in the dike" effect. The structure of blind obedience to external authority was undermined.

In sum, the result of the changes of Vatican II was that Catholics began to believe that sin was perhaps not an objective phenomenon out there for all time, determined by some external unchanging authority, but highly situational and subject to legitimate redefinition over time. Given hierarchical approval of people taking responsibility for their own behavior in the matter of fast and abstinence, it is not too surprising that Catholics decided that they were in a better position than the hierarchy to judge what was and was not sinful in other matters, especially in matters of personal sexual conduct. The distinction the Church hierarchy would make between a Church law (on fast and abstinence) designed as a discipline, and the natural law argument (on contraceptive birth control) presumably derived from right reasoning, has been lost on the laity.

Increasing Pluralism Within the American Catholic Church

Within a decade of Vatican II, it was obvious that Catholics were rapidly becoming more like Protestants and Jews in their behaviors regarding churchgoing, family planning, divorce, and kinship (Greeley, 1976; D'Antonio, 1980, 1983,1985; Seidler, 1986; Roof and Mckinney, 1987). Now Catholics were increasingly found in the same levels of occupational status, educational achievement and income as Protestants and Jews.

An inevitable product of assimilation into all circles of American life was new reflection by Catholics on the Church's moral teachings. Not all agreed with the teachings or with each other's critiques, and lines of cleavage began to appear which resembled the lines in Protestantism and Judaism. Thus, for example, Orthodox Jews, fundamentalist Protestants and traditional Catholics may all oppose abortion, at the same time that progressive Catholics, Protestants and Jews support the right to abortion under at least some circumstances. This moral clustering across denominational lines also occurs on divorce, birth control, and other issues such as capital punishment. American Catholicism (just like other religious communities) is being reshaped by deeper currents within American culture. Certain factors within the Church acted to promote the process.

1. The American hierarchy was slow to come to grips with the implications of Vatican II. It was also slow to respond to the movements going on in American society. It was slow, for instance, to take a position on Vietnam, even as it was slow to recognize the religious and spiritual significance of Rev. Martin Luther King, Jr. and the Civil Rights Movement. It never felt comfortable with the women's movement or the students' movement. Its response to the laity's rebellion against *Humanae Vitae* was highly defensive. (Ruether, 1987: Ch.2). Fichter (1977) was one of the first to observe that the Catholic Church was experiencing a revolution from below in that the laity were thinking moral, political and social issues through for themselves and no longer waiting for direction from the hierarchy. Fee, Greeley and associates (1981) documented this in their studies on *Young Catholics* and *The Religious Imagination*. Thus, the Church's traditional response to the Birth Control Debate had the unintended effect of weakening its authority over the laity, just as society and the government's responses to the several

protest movements diminished their aura of legitimacy over many citizens. The resulting loss of belief in the legitimacy of church and state led to varying degrees of polarization, pluralism, and a kind of privatism or individualism that further eroded commitment to larger social organizations.

2. While *Humanae Vitae* had a negative impact and alienated many Catholics from the Church, other actions of Vatican II were more positive. The movement to revise the Code of Canon Law was initiated by Pope John XXIII at the same time that he announced the Second Vatican Council. The revised Code of Canon Law legitimizes the expansion of lay participation in the Church. For example, Canon 129 states: "In accord with the prescriptions of the law, those who have received sacred orders are capable of the power of governance, which exists in the Church by divine institution and is also called the power of jurisdiction. Lay members of the Christian faithful can cooperate in the exercise of this power in accord with the norm of law." Canon 228 also states: "Qualified lay persons are capable of assuming from their sacred pastors those ecclesiastical offices and functions which they are able to exercise in accord with the prescriptions of law. Lay persons who excel in the necessary knowledge, prudence, and uprightness are capable of assisting the pastors of the Church as experts or advisors; they can do so even in councils, in accord with the norm of law" (1983: 41,77).

Thus, while the use of phrases like ". . . can cooperate . . ." and ". . . are capable of . . ." allows the clergy and hierarchy an out, new roles were gradually offered to the laity. The reality is that though uneven, change has taken place, and laity now occupy positions of some importance in local and diocesan offices. And since it is difficult to particularize and constrain change once the process is underway, it is not surprising that more and more features of Catholic life became caught up in the process.

3. Perhaps the most surprising development in the past decade has been the American bishops' new and controversial stands on issues of national and international importance, namely, their peace pastoral, the

pastoral on the American economy, and the most recent pastoral draft on women's concerns. Less widely heralded but also significant has been the effort of Cardinal Joseph Bernardin to articulate a "Consistent Life Ethic," an approach to the question of the sacredness of human life that links concerns about prenatal life with lives of poverty, deaths of innocents in war, capital punishment and the threat of nuclear war. (Peterson and Takayama, 1984). Thus, in sharp contrast to their behavior during the 1960s, many American bishops have become proponents of social and value change. The peace and economy pastorals in particular have been warmly received in progressive circles and roundly criticized by conservatives.

An important element in these pastorals is that the bishops have invited the laity and all others interested to take part in the debate with them. They did not attempt to issue an edict from on high, in the traditional hierarchical manner, to be obeyed without question. Even Cardinal Bernardin, in his statement on a *Consistent Life Ethic* (1983), did not present it as an edict but as an issue for serious discussion. This seems like a major concession to rational discourse and the recognition of the value of intellectual autonomy.

4. A consequence of these changes is the effort by some of the laity and clergy to make open debate normative, and extend it to the abortion issue. The current state of the struggle between obedience and dissent in the Church is nowhere better seen than in the abortion question. (In earlier eras, the focus was on divorce and birth control.) The majority of the American hierarchy, strongly backed by the Vatican, is trying to assert traditional authority. Rome is saying that there is no room for dissent on the abortion issue, that is, no room for public dissent from the official position of the Church hierarchy that abortion is always gravely wrong.

Thirty years ago, at the time of Lenski's study, there was no public dissent in the Church; Catholics who disagreed with the official position either remained silent, were silenced by the Church, left the Church voluntarily, or were excommunicated. If they accepted the teachings and then sinned, they went to confession where they repented, were given absolution, and restored to the "good graces of Mother Church." Today many Catholics resist certain teachings (whether on birth control, capital punishment, or capitalism), defend their right to rational discourse, challenge the teachings and the teachers, and still insist on continuing to be part of the Church (Ruether, 1987:63 ff).

At one level, the current struggle focuses on the nature and consequences of authority in the Church. Prior to Vatican II, the Church was considered to be essentially traditional, hierarchic and monolithic. The pope was seen as the ultimate source of authority on earth, having a direct link with Christ through apostolic succession. That authority was grounded in a two-thousand year line of tradition, built on centuries of scholarly and dogmatic interpretations of the writings of the original apostles, and of the meaning of the Old Testament in the light of Christ's life. Over time the interpretations themselves have taken on a sacred quality, and they are now commonly said by conservative Church leaders to be inerrant.

Is Democratization of the Church Likely to Continue?

Factions in the Church today argue about the place and nature of reason. It is important to recognize the difference between the way the Church leaders have come to use what they call "right reason" to reach their conclusions about what is morally wrong and right, and the use of reason in the modern sense of legal-rational discourse. The former uses reason to arrive at truths already known or believed; the only doubt is in the quality of the reasoning. The latter, as reflecting both science and the kind of rational discourse characteristic of a democratic society, uses reason to help discover relationships, causes and probable truths, but with the recognition that the truth is not necessarily known beforehand and that it is always subject to change and modification as knowledge grows. Most Church leaders have made their uneasy peace with this kind of reason as it applies to science, but many reject it when applied to social behavior that involves religious beliefs and teachings such as those on birth control, divorce and sexuality. They have been especially reluctant to recognize the experience of the laity, the consensus of the faithful, as it were, in these matters.

Conservative church leaders insist that not only are the teachings inerrant, but that right-thinking people, Catholics or not, should be able to come to the correct conclusions about the moral rightness or wrongness of an act, such as birth control, since the teaching is really in conformity with the natural law. At the same time, church leaders insist that Catholics are free to form their own conscience, and that they must follow it. If Catholics follow the teachings of the Church , they will always be doing the right thing. At the same time the leaders acknowledge that in matters not involving overtly stated infallible teachings, individuals may dissent, but how far this dissent can be taken is now subject to debate. With regard to the abortion issue, for example, church leaders have been most rigorous in trying to proscribe public dissent by people with official religious ties to the Church. Among the most noteworthy have been the cases of Fr. Charles Curran and the 22 nuns who signed the *New York Times* article in October, 1984. U.S. Church leaders also brought tremendous public pressure to bear against Democratic vice-presidential candidate Geraldine Ferraro in the 1984 presidential campaign because she defended her right to support the current legal status of abortion in the United States. And in the opening pages of Chapter 4, we cite the case of Mrs. Mary Ann Sorrentino, who was excommunicated because of her refusal to relinquish her role as Executive Director of Planned Parenthood of Rhode Island. These actions have been taken despite the fact that the Pope has never declared the Church's teaching on abortion to be infallible.

It can be fairly argued that the bishops (or at least many of them worldwide) tried to establish a more rational, democratic authority model during Vatican II. The Council document on the *Church in the Modern World* moved in that direction, as did the debate on the pill and birth control. Had Pope Paul VI accepted the report of the majority of the Birth Control Commission, we might be able to say today that significant movement toward a more democratic authority structure had taken place and could be expected to continue in the future. But while Paul VI did many things to encourage a more democratic, rational approach, he moved back to tradition and to patriarchal authoritarianism on the birth control issue, and so the struggle between democratic and authoritarian forces continues, with John Paul II clearly aligned with the latter.

Is a return to a 19th-century anti-modernist, patriarchal, autocratic church organization possible today? Can there be a revival of a Church with an overwhelming majority of praying, paying and obeying adherents? Certainly, John Paul II has many supporters in his efforts to restore papal authority. In addition to members of the Roman Curia like Cardinal Ratzinger, such organizations as Opus Dei, some Right to Life groups, and many conservative cardinals are available to defend his teachings. And with his most recent appointments of new cardinals, the conservatives now hold a majority among U.S. cardinals.

The Pope, of course, has the authority to excommunicate all those who dissent openly on issues like abortion, divorce and birth control. Such an action could well reduce the size of the American Catholic population by at least one-half. For public-relations purposes alone, it seems doubtful that the leaders in the American Church would advise him to move in that direction. And despite growing evidence that Catholics are contributing less financially even as their incomes continue to rise, there would no doubt be significant additional damage to the Church's financial structure should the Vatican demand such orthodoxy. The pope's reluctant excommunication of the reactionary Archbishop LeFebvre, in June, 1988, only after he publicly disobeyed the pope and consecrated four new bishops to his conservative movement, suggests that the pope will move slowly to avoid schism on either the extreme left or right.

The issue of personal autonomy and voluntary association is now focusing on Catholic colleges and universities. Rome would like to force them into a more obedient mode, as indicated in the draft document issued from the Vatican which would put Catholic colleges and universities under control of local bishops (*Washington Post,* March 28, 1986:A2) Included in the draft are such provisions as these:

The bishop could declare a school "no longer Catholic" if "the Catholic character . . . continues to be compromised in a serious way." Not only are faculty members to be chosen for their "doctrinal integrity and uprightness of life" as much as for academic qualification, but the proposal also states that teachers "who lack these requirements are to be dismissed."

In a twelve-page critique sent to Rome, presidents of 235 Catholic colleges and universities expressed strong dissent from this proposal. They tried to make clear to the Vatican how important to American higher education is the principle of academic freedom, and how the Vatican proposal would undermine that principle. Furthermore, given the financial dependence of the leading Catholic universities on the federal government for research and student aid, and on gifts from alumni and private foundations, the implementation of such a proposal would be disastrous for Catholic colleges and universities in the United States. So for a variety of reasons, these colleges and universities are becoming increasingly independent of the Vatican, as they take on the characteristics of voluntary associations that stress intellectual autonomy as a major outcome of a liberal education.

In this regard, the tension between autocratic rule and personal autonomy is exemplified in the struggle between the Vatican and Fr. Charles Curran, a tenured moral theologian at the Catholic University of America. The scholarly writings of Fr. Curran had been under Vatican investigation for years, ever since Curran had been identified as one of the leaders in the American Catholic Theologians' protest against *Humanae Vitae.* When he refused in 1987 to retract his writings on sexual morality and divorce, he was expelled from the theological faculty of the Catholic University. Since the Theology Department of Catholic University is chartered by the Vatican, it is subject to Roman authority. "The issue," says Fr. Curran , "is whether a Catholic scholar can dissent from authoritative but non-infallible teachings of the Church." According to the present edict from the Vatican, he cannot dissent and still carry the title of Catholic Theologian under the charter of the Vatican. The event provides a somber preview of what life would be like were the Vatican able to bring all Catholic colleges and universities under control of the Church hierarchy.

In all these events we find that the efforts of individuals to be intellectually autonomous confront the traditional hierarchical organization of the Roman Catholic Church. Given the central place of intellectual autonomy in America, the clash between church leaders and the American laity seems to have been inevitable. The opposing forces at times appear to be irreconcilable. Of course, it may be some consolation to recall that St. Thomas Aquinas was silenced, called a heretic, censured and condemned by church leaders before they changed their minds and made him a doctor of the Church.

Looking to the Future

What then is the future of the Roman Catholic Church in America? The irony is that while clergy like Curran and progressive Catholic lay leaders have been trying to establish the right of responsible intellectual autonomy within the institutional structure of the Church, millions of Americans have been moving in a different direction—toward self-absorption in satisfying personal needs and wants. Americans' quest for autonomy in the past decade seems less focused on a responsible concern for the common good, and more and more on meeting narrowly defined selfish needs. The 1980s in America have been characterized as an era of privatism and self-absorption. In the eyes of Bellah, et al. (1985): "Our present radical individualism is in part a justified reaction against communities and practices that were irrationally restrictive." But Bellah and his colleagues also remind us that unrestrained individualism threatens the welfare of both the individual and the society. They warn us that we must restrain individualism now just as it was restrained by

Americans 150 years ago. As we cited early in this chapter, polity and religion were the crucial restraints on individualism then. The question arises whether they can become that again in our time.

The challenge within the Catholic religion is to foster mechanisms of interaction between the bishops and the laity that will lead Catholics beyond private concerns of personal moral conduct. The laity, including many conservatives, have spent much time since Vatican II freeing themselves from narrrow church strictures on matters having to do with sexuality and marriage. That has created a focus on personal behavior. And it has coincided with the post-Watergate, post-Vietnam, post-Civil Rights mood of privatism, "what's in it for me?" that has dominated American society since the mid-1970's.

While our data provide more than adequate evidence to support Fichter, Greeley and other researchers, our study does not suggest that the personal autonomy sought and now achieved by so many Catholics means that they are turning their backs on Church participation. They are not saying "my way or no way!" Rather, as we will show in the coming pages, they are asking to be included in the decision-making process.

Just as Bellah and others have argued that community structures and the cultural patterns that undergird them have been weakened by the events of the past two decades in American society, so is it that the formal structure and cultural supports of the Catholic Church in the United States seem to have been weakened. Progressives believe that the weakening has been necessary because the structure is outmoded, depending as it does on decrees from above. They understand the Church as the people of God. Their aim is to reform the structure, to make themselves an integral part of the Church's decision-making.

Conservatives believe that the old structure was essentially sound, and that Vatican II unnecessarily undid it. Their understanding of the Church is hierarchic, autocratic and centralized. Our study of the U.S. Catholic laity in 1987 attempts to show where the American Catholic laity as a whole stand on this issue. It was designed to explore the Catholic laity's desire to be part of a more collegial, democratic Catholic Church on the one hand, or to continue to support the more autocratic, hierarchic model on the other. We turn now to the results of our study.

References

Bell, Daniel. 1967. "Toward a Communal Society." *Life,* May 12. New York: Time, Life, Inc.

Bellah, Robert N., Richard Madsen, William M. Sullivan, Ann Swidler, and Steven M. Tipton. 1985. *Habits of the Heart.* Berkeley, CA: University of California Press.

Bernardin, Joseph Cardinal. 1983. *The Seamless Garment, Discussion on a Consistent Life Ethic.* Kansas City, MO: Sheed & Ward, National Catholic Reporter Publishing Co.

Canon Law Society of America. 1983. *The Code of Canon Law: Latin-English.* Washington, DC: Canon Law Society.

D'Antonio, William V. 1980. "The Family and Religion: Exploring a Changing Relationship." *Journal for the Scientific Study of Religion.* 19:2,89-104.

_____. and Joan Aldous (eds.). 1983. *Families and Religions: Conflict and Change in Modern Society.* Beverly Hills: Sage Publications.

_____. 1985. "The American Catholic Family: Signs of Cohesion and Polarization," *Journal of Marriage and the Family,* May, 395-405.

Ellis, John Tracy. 1956. *American Catholics and the Intellectual Life.* Chicago: Heritage Foundation.

Fee, Joan L., Andrew M. Greeley, William C. McCready and Teresa A. Sullivan. 1981. *Young Catholics*. New York: Sadlier.

Fichter, Joseph H. 1973. *One-Man Research: Reminiscences of a Catholic Sociologist*. New York: John Wiley and Sons.

_____. 1977. "Restructuring Catholicism." *Sociological Analysis* 38:2, 154-164.

Glock, Charles Y. and Rodney Stark. 1965. *Religion and Society in Tension*. New York: Rand McNally.

Greeley, Andrew M. 1976 . *Catholic Schools in a Declining Church*. Kansas City: Sheed, Andrews and McMeel.

_____. 1981. *The Religious Imagination*. New York: Sadlier.

_____. 1985. *American Catholics Since the Council: An Unauthorized Report*. Chicago: Thomas More.

Hoge, Dean. 1987. *The Future of Catholic Leadership*. Kansas City: Sheed and Ward.

Hoyt, Robert G.(ed.). 1968. *The Birth Control Debate*. Kansas City: *National Catholic Reporter*.

Lenski, Gerhard. 1963. *The Religious Factor: A Sociologist's Inquiry*. New York: Doubleday/Anchor Books.

O'Dea, Thomas. 1958. *American Catholic Dilemma: An Inquiry into the Intellectual Life*. New York: Sheed and Ward.

Peterson, Larry R. and K. Peter Takayama. 1984. "Religious Commitment and Conservatism: Toward Understanding an Elusive Relationship." *Sociological Analysis*. 45:4, 355-371.

Roof, Wade Clark and William McKinney. 1987. *American Mainline Religion*. New Brunswick: Rutgers University Press.

Ruether, Rosemary Radford. 1987. *Contemporary Roman Catholicism:Crisis and Challenges*. Kansas City: Sheed and Ward.

Seidler, John. 1986. "Contested Accomodation: The Catholic Church as a Special Case of Social Change." *Social Forces* 64:4 (June), 847-874.

Tocqueville, Alexis de. 1984. *Democracy in America*. New York: New American Library. Edited by Richard D. Heffner.

2.

American Catholics: A Profile of Changing Involvement

What if all Catholic Americans had a family reunion in 1987? And what if someone took a family picture? Who would be in the picture?

The data in Table 2.1 give us some answers. One of the first things we might notice is that the vast majority of the people in the picture are white; the rest are Hispanics, Blacks, and Asians in that order. All the age groups are represented: there are about as many older people (55 and over) as there are younger ones (34 or less). Just over half of the people are women (52 percent). Sixty-two percent are currently married; 15 percent had been married before but were now divorced. widowed, or separated; the other 22 percent have never been married. Most people (44 percent) are from cities with a million or more people in them, and many others also are from other fairly large cities.

Eighty percent of the people in the picture are high school graduates and half of them have been to college (20 percent are college graduates). Half have attended Catholic grade schools; one-quarter have gone to Catholic high schools; and eight percent have gone to Catholic colleges. Nearly one-quarter are in high-status white-collar occupations; another

Table 2.1
American Catholics (percent)

Race	
White	86
Hispanic	10*
Black	3
Asian	1
Other, refused	1
Marital Status	
Married	62
Never Married	22
Divorced, Widowed, Separated	15
Age	
55 or older	27
45-54	12
35-44	18
25-34	26
18-24	17
Sex	
Male	48
Female	52
City Size	
Less than 25,000	29
25,000-249,999	14
250,000-999,999	13
One million or more	44

(continued)

Education

At least some graduate/professional schooling	8
College graduate	12
Some college, vocational school	20
High school graduate	40
Some high school or less	21

Catholic Education

Grade school	52
High school	25
College	8

Occupation

Professional (e.g., lawyer, teacher, nurse)	14
Manager, executive, or official (e.g., business, government)	6
Business owner (e.g., store, plumbing contractor)	3
Clerical or office worker (e.g., secretary)	12
Sales (e.g., clerk in store, sales representative)	6
Service worker (e.g., police, fire, barber)	8
Skilled tradesman (e.g., baker, electrician)	10
Semiskilled worker (e.g., assembly line, driver)	6
Laborer (e.g., construction, longshoreman)	4

Income

$40,000 or more	19
$30,000-$39,999	13
$20,000-$29,999	19
$10,000-$19,999	20
Under $10,000	12
No answer (don't know, refused)	18

---

*An underestimation based on sampling procedures. See text for explanation.

18 percent are in clerical or sales work; and 28 percent are in blue collar jobs. About one-third have family incomes of $30,000 or more; 39 percent earn between $10,000 and $29,999; and 12 percent have incomes of $10,000 or less.

The Catholic population has experienced many changes over the last 25 or 30 years. They are no longer the working-class immigrants depicted in so many earlier family pictures. After scoring impressive gains in almost all areas of socio-economic achievement, Catholics now rank among the more highly educated and affluent religious groups in the country. Many also have moved from the central city neighborhoods where their parents and grandparents lived to more spacious and comfortable suburbs (Greeley, 1977).

There also have been enormous changes within the Church itself. In the pre-Vatican II 1950s, the Church expected its members to be highly involved and to support the Church. Catholics were expected to attend Mass every Sunday and all Holy Days, go to confession regularly, eat no meat on Fridays, support the Church financially, and participate in a variety of devotional activities (retreats, novenas, and rosaries) designed to foster "spirituality." Sanctions against those who violated these norms were severe: missing Mass, eating meat on Friday, and not making one's "Easter duty" were all mortal sins.

Since Vatican II (1962-65), Church norms and expectations have changed dramatically. Some of the strictest norms (e.g., not eating meat on Fridays) were discontinued. Others were modified: now Catholics are "encouraged" to go to confession and to attend Mass regularly; they are no longer told that failure to do so is a mortal sin.

What have all these changes done to Catholics' involvement in the Church? How religious are American Catholics today? How actively involved are they in the Church? Are some Catholics more involved than others? Which Catholics are most or least involved? How does the current level of Catholic commitment compare with earlier periods? Has involvement in the Church increased or decreased in recent years? What do current trends portend for the future? Should we expect more or less involvement in the years ahead?

In this chapter, we look at each of these questions in light of the evidence from our survey. First, we will describe the current patterns of involvement, including a look at the kinds of Catholics who are most and least involved in the Church today. Then, we'll examine trends in Catholic commitment, looking back over the last 30 to 40 years and then looking into the future. We'll conclude with some thoughts about what these findings mean for the Church in the years ahead.

Measuring Involvement

Our approach assumes that religious involvement is both subjective and behavioral: it is a matter of attitude and action, personal feeling and public participation (Davidson and Knudsen, 1977; Davidson, Knudson, and Lerch, 1983).

To tap the more subjective aspects of Catholics' involvement in the Church, we asked our respondents two questions:

1. How important is the Catholic Church to you personally?

2. Now I would like you to imagine a scale from 1 to 7. At point 1 is the statement, "I would never leave the Catholic Church." At point 7 is the statement, "Yes, I might leave the Catholic Church." Where would you place yourself on that scale?

We asked the respondents three questions about their participation in religious activities.

1. How often do you attend Mass?

2. How much money would you say your household contributes to the Catholic Church each year, not counting tuition?

3. How often do you read the Bible? (This has not been a traditional indicator of Catholic commitment; but in accordance with the ecumenical thrust of Vatican II, Catholic leaders have been encouraging laity to read the Bible more often. We wanted to see to what extent Catholics were adopting this traditionally Protestant form of religious expression).

In the next section, we look at the data concerning all five of these items.

Present Patterns

Overall, Catholics say the Church is a rather important part of their lives, and they are unlikely to leave the Church (see Table 2.2).[1] They attend Mass regularly and contribute $250 or more to the Church each year. Though clergy now put far more emphasis on scripture reading among lay people than they did in the pre-Vatican II period, the laity still do not read the Bible with any frequency.

Within this overall context, there is a good deal of variation. Only 13 percent of American Catholics say the Church is the most important part of their lives, but another 74 percent feel the Church is "quite important" or "among the most important parts" of their lives. Fifty-five percent say they would never consider leaving the Church, though 16 percent say they can conceive of circumstances under which they might leave. Forty-four percent of Catholics attend Mass at least every week. Another 30 percent attend on the average of two or three times a month. About one-quarter of Catholics seldom, if ever, attend. Forty-eight percent gave more than $250 to the Church in 1986. About one-third of Catholics

---

1. These dimensions of involvement tend to be correlated, though not perfectly. For example, 84 percent of Catholics who say the Church is the most important part of their lives also attend Mass weekly, compared to 31 percent for those who say the Church is "quite important," and zero percent among those who say the Church is "not very important." Eighty-seven percent of those who say the Church is "most important" also are unwilling to leave it, compared to 45 percent for those who say the Church is "quite important," and 22 percent of those who say it is "not very important."

gave $100 or less. Finally, most Catholics do not read the Bible on a regular basis, though some (about 17 percent) do.

These findings are very similar to those contained in other recent surveys of American Catholics (e.g., Greeley, 1977). The only differences worth noting concern the ethnic composition of Catholics in our sample and our finding that only 44 percent of Catholics attend Mass weekly.

We did not realize it until after the survey was done, but the Gallup agency—which conducted the telephone poll for us—employed the same sampling procedure it usually uses in its "omnibus" surveys. That procedure includes a policy of only interviewing English-speaking adults. This fact has two implications: our sample underestimates the number of Hispanic Catholics (whereas census data indicate that Hispanics comprise about 25 percent of all Catholics, only 10 percent of our sample is Hispanic), but it allows us to make comparisons with other Gallup surveys (several of which are very helpful bases for plotting trends in Catholic involvement).

Also, other surveys done during the 1980s indicate that between 50 and 52 percent of Catholics attend Mass weekly. Our data say only 44 percent. There are two possible explanations for this difference: sampling error (which can be plus or minus four percentage points in surveys of this type) and/or slightly different wording of the question pertaining to frequency of Mass attendance. It is not clear whether our data are slightly biased or represent first indications of even lower rates of Mass attendance (see later sections of this chapter for more on such trends).

Explaining Variations

Given these variations, we wondered why some Catholics are more involved than others. Our family picture showed that Catholic lay people live in a variety of social contexts, each of which includes values and self-interests derived from a combination of ancestral experiences, which

Table 2.2

Overall Patterns of Involvement (percent)

Indicators of Involvement	Percent
Importance of the Church to you?	
Most important part of my life	13
Among the most important parts of my life	36
Quite important, but so are other areas	38
Not terribly important	9
Not very important	3
Likelihood of leaving the Church	
1 (would never leave)	55
2	9
3	9
4	10
5	7
6	4
7 (might leave)	6
Mass attendance	
At least once a week	44
Almost every week	30
Seldom, never	25
Contributions	
Over $500	22
$251-500	26
$101-250	19
$1-100	24
None	9
Reading the Bible	
Daily, at least once a week	17
Almost every week	13
Seldom, never	70

have been passed down over generations, and contemporary experiences related to one's personal lot in life. These different social contexts foster different patterns of involvement in the Church.

Four social contexts seem to be especially important sources of commitment: region, occupation, Catholic schooling, and ethnicity (see Table 2.3).

Region

There were significant regional differences on all five dimensions of involvement. Overall, Catholics living in the Southwest (i.e., Arkansas, Louisiana, Oklahoma, and Texas) tend to be most involved in the Church. Sixty-two percent say the Church is important; 55 percent attend Mass regularly; and 23 percent (which is high for Catholics) read the Bible on a regular basis.

After the Southwest, the most involved regions are West Central, Southeast, Middle Atlantic, New England, and East Central (in that order). Each of these regions has its own pattern of involvement. For example, Catholics in the Middle Atlantic states are about average in all five of the areas we examined, while people in the Southeast are somewhat less likely to leave the Church but also are less regular in Mass attendance and give less money to the Church.

Catholics in the Rocky Mountain and Pacific regions tend to be least involved, though their rates of involvement are not dramatically different from the national average on each dimension.

Occupation

Catholics toward the top of America's occupational ladder are somewhat more involved than people in lower-status jobs. Laity in two white-collar occupations (business owners, and clerical and sales workers) tend to be most active. These two groups are the most frequent Mass attenders, among the biggest contributors (along with managers and professionals), and among the most frequent Bible readers (along with managers again). Business people are most inclined to say they would never leave the Church. White-collar workers (especially clerical workers and people in sales) are most likely to say the Church is important. In general, blue-collar workers tend to be less involved, though they are not inclined to leave the Church.

Amount of Catholic Education

The amount of *Catholic* schooling one has seems even more important than the total number of years a person has been in school. In general, the more Catholic education one has, the more involved one tends to be. The only items where this generalization does not hold up have to do with the likelihood of leaving the Church and reading the Bible.

Ethnicity

Everyone knows that various ethnic groups have their own versions of the Catholic faith. There are all sorts of accounts of how different Irish Catholics are from Italian Catholics, and how different German Catholics are from Hispanics. While some of these differences have diminished with the "Americanization" of Catholics, our data indicate that ethnicity remains a factor in the extent and nature of Catholics' involvement in the Church.

Ethnic differences are most pronounced in the importance Catholics attach to the Church (Poles are highest; Germans and Hispanics, lowest), Mass attendance (Poles are most frequent, Hispanics attend least often), and financial contributions (Germans are most generous; Hispanics give the least).

****

Five other factors (gender, marital status, race, education, and income) were somewhat less important overall, though each had effects which should not be overlooked.

Gender

Our data support the now well-documented finding that women are more religiously involved than men. Female Catholics are significantly more likely to say the Church is important and to attend Mass regularly, somewhat less likely to leave the Church, and somewhat more likely to read the Bible. The differences between the sexes' financial contributions are minimal.

Marital Status

Families have been the backbone of the Church, with married couples traditionally exhibiting more religious fervor than single people. Our data tend to support this pattern. Married Catholics are significantly more likely to attend Mass and contribute to the Church financially, and somewhat more likely to say the Church is important. There are no appreciable differences between the two groups in the other two areas of involvement (likelihood of leaving the Church and Bible reading).

Race

In light of the dominant role Whites have played in the Church over the years, and Blacks' subordination, it is not surprising to find that Whites are more likely to say they are unwilling to leave the Church, and are more inclined to attend Mass on a regular basis. However, we were impressed to find that Blacks are somewhat more likely than Whites to say the Church is important, and somewhat more likely to donate over $250 a year to the Church. The races read the Bible with about equal frequency.

Amount of Education

There have been long-standing debates about the effects education has on religious commitment. Does it foster commitment, or jeopardize it? Our data suggest its effects may depend on what type of commitment one is talking about. The higher one's educational level, the less willing one is to leave the Church, but—also—the less likely one is to contribute to the Church financially. Education has no appreciable effect on the other dimensions of church involvement.

Income

Though occupational status has rather consistent effects on involvement, the effects of family income were less consistent. The lower the income of Catholic families, the less likely they are to leave the Church, but the less money they give to the Church. Income has no appreciable effect on the other three dimensions of involvement.

Recent Trends

How do today's rates of commitment compare with those of 25 or 30 years ago? Have the social and religious changes described at the outset of this chapter had much effect on Catholics' involvement in the Church? And, if so, what kind of effect have they had?

It is impossible to compare data for all five of the measures used in this chapter. However, data on two of them—the importance of religion and frequency of Mass attendance—point to the same conclusion: there has been an overall decline in involvement among Catholics. Data from other Gallup surveys (e.g., 1985) indicate that in 1952, 83 percent of Catholics said that religion was a "very important" part of their lives. The percentage dropped to 51 by 1978 before rebounding slightly (between 53 and 56 percent) during the 1980s. Data in Table 2.2 are consistent with these other data: about half of the Catholics in our sample say the Church is the "most important part" of their lives or "among the most

Table 2.3

Extent of Religious Involvement by Social Context
(percent "High")*

	Subjective Involvement**		Behavioral Involvement**		
	Importance of Church	Unlikely to leave	Mass Attend.	Contri-butions	Reading Bible
All Catholics	49	55	44	48	17
More Important Factors					
Region					
Southwest	62	60	55	44	23
West Central	51	54	50	63	21
Southeast	52	64	29	39	21
Mid. Atlantic	50	57	47	46	19
New England	45	60	45	48	9
East Central	44	56	41	52	19
Pacific	45	48	37	42	23
Rockies	45	40	38	46	19
Occupation					
Bus. Owner	38	78	54	62	32
Manager	40	36	39	55	21
Professional	48	41	49	51	16
Cler/Sales	50	54	55	47	20
Service	45	39	28	37	10
Skilled	34	54	29	39	16
Semi-skilled	48	54	27	42	16
Laborer	27	49	28	47	12
Catholic Education					
Three levels	69	60	56	60	14
Two	54	53	53	58	19
One	45	60	40	41	18
None	46	53	41	45	21
Ethnicity					
Polish	62	63	50	46	26
Irish	56	53	48	48	20
Italian	50	62	44	46	19
German	45	57	48	56	15
Hispanic	45	53	30	39	21
Other	44	53	42	46	19

(continued)

	Subjective Involvement**		Behavioral Involvement**		
	Importance of Church	Unlikely to leave	Mass Attend.	Contri- butions	Reading Bible
Less Important Factors					
Gender					
Female	58	61	52	47	22
Male	39	50	35	49	15
Martial Status					
Married	53	75	50	52	19
Single	43	74	34	39	18
Race					
Whilte	49	57	46	49	19
Black	55	35	34	54	18
Education					
< H.S.	54	75	42	38	17
High School	50	55	48	46	22
> H.S.	46	45	42	53	17
Income					
> $40,000	45	45	44	61	19
$20-40,000	48	48	44	49	18
< $20,000	51	67	44	40	21

*Differences of 12 percentage points or more are statistically significant at .05 level.

**High Importance = Most important part of my life, or among the most important parts of my life.
Highly Unlikely to Leave = 1.
High Mass Attendance = At least once a week.
High Contributions = Donations of $250 or more.
High Reading the Bible = At least once a week.

important parts." (According to other Gallup polls, the percentages for Protestants are slightly higher but reveal the same downward trend.)

The data in Figure 2.1 indicate that most Catholics attended Mass every week in 1958. By 1963, that percentage had declined to about 71 percent. In 1968, only 65 percent of Catholics were attending Mass weekly. By the mid 1970s, the percentage of weekly attenders had dropped to 55. In 1983, only 52 percent of Catholics attended in the previous week. Our 1987 survey used a slightly different question, which explains the variation in the findings.

Our data suggest the dramatic religious changes accompanying Vatican II are at least partly responsible for this decline. As Table 2.3 indicates, the decline began during the early 1960s, right around the time of Vatican II. And, according to the data in Table 2.4, people who have embraced the more progressive views of the post-Vatican II period regarding liturgical and doctrinal matters have consistently lower rates of Mass attendance than those who hold to more traditional standards. For example, 74 percent of Catholics who took the more traditional view

Figure 2.1

Trend in Weekly Mass Attendance, 1958-1987

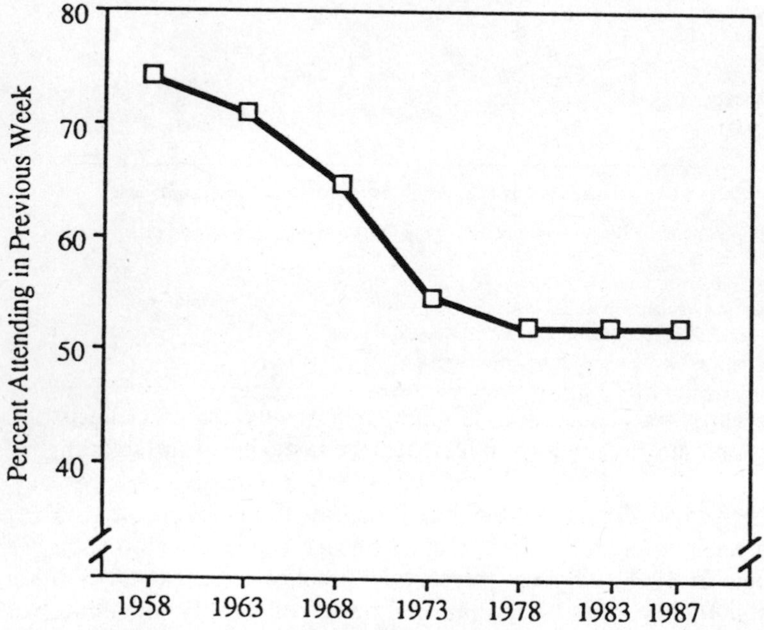

Source: Gallup (1978; 1985; 1987).

Table 2.4

Frequency of Mass Attendance by Conceptions of Being a Good Catholic (percent)

Standards	Percent Attending Mass Regularly
Liturgical Standards	
Mass Attendance	
1. Traditional: one cannot be a "good Catholic" without attending Mass regularly	74
2. Progressive: one can be a "good Catholic" without attending regularly	33
Confession	
1. Traditional: one cannot be a "good Catholic" without going to confession at least once a year	52
2. Progressive: one can be a "good Catholic" without annual confession	39
Easter Communion	
1. Traditional: one cannot be a "good Catholic" without going to communion at Easter	56
2. Progressive: one can be a "good Catholic" without Easter communion	36
Doctrinal Standards	
Birth Control	
1. Traditional: one cannot be a "good Catholic" without believing in the Church's ban on birth control	61
2. Progressive: one can be a "good Catholic" and disagree with the Church's view of birth control	36
Abortion	
1. Traditional: one cannot be a "good Catholic" without accepting the Church's view on abortion	69
2. Progressive: one can be a "good Catholic" and disagree with the Church's opposition to abortion	29

that going to Mass on a regular basis is an integral part of being a "good Catholic" attended Mass regularly, compared to only one-third of Catholics who took the more progressive view that one can be a "good Catholic" without attending Mass regularly. Also, 61 percent of

Catholics who agreed with the more traditional view that accepting the Church's position on birth control is part of being a "good Catholic" attended Mass regularly, compared with only 36 percent of those with the more progressive view that one can be a "good Catholic" and still disagree with the Church's teaching on birth control.

Greeley (1977, 1986) has argued that Pope Paul VI's encyclical *Humanae Vitae* angered many Catholics and precipitated a crisis of confidence, which led to lower levels of involvement. Our data suggest that the negative response to *Humanae Vitae* may account for the especially sharp drop in Mass attendance between 1968 and the mid 1970s, but the decline began several years before the encyclical was issued and is related to a much larger set of issues. The encyclical did not initiate the decline; it only made matters worse.

Future Trends

Given today's lower level of involvement, it is only natural to ask about the future. Are we likely to see even lower levels of involvement in the years ahead? Is there any reason to expect a leveling off—or even a reversal—of present trends?

One way to address these issues is to see how young Catholics today are thinking and acting and to make some projections based on these patterns. This "cohort" approach assumes that, all other things being equal, the religious attitudes and behavior patterns which young Catholics develop during their formative years tend to persist in their middle years and when they are older. If young Catholics are more active in the Church than the older generation, there is likely to be an increase in the overall extent of involvement as the younger generation replaces the older one. If, on the other hand, the younger generation is less active in the Church, the overall rate of involvement is likely to decline as the younger cohort replaces the older, more active, one.

Table 2.5 indicates that, all other things being equal, the trend is toward even lower rates of involvement in the years ahead. Only 37 percent of young Catholics (18 to 29 years of age) say the Church is an important part of their lives, compared to 45 percent of 30-54 year olds and 66 percent of Catholics who are 55 years of age or older. Only 42 percent of young Catholics say they are unlikely to leave the Church, compared to half of middle-aged Catholics and 80 percent of older Catholics.

Participation rates reveal much the same pattern. Only 29 percent of young Catholics attend Mass weekly, compared to 43 percent of 30-54 year olds and 63 percent of people 55 and over. Only 31 percent contributed $250 or more in 1986, compared to 53 percent of middle-aged Catholics and 57 percent of older Catholics. Finally, only 14 percent

Table 2.5

Involvement by Age (percent "High")

Age	Subjective Involvement		Behavioral Involvement		
	Importance of Church	Unlikely to leave	Mass Attend.	Contri- butions	Reading Bible
55 or over	66	80	53	57	23
30-54	45	50	43	53	20
29 or less	37	42	29	31	14

read the Bible on a regular basis, compared to 20 percent of Catholics between 30 and 54 years of age and 23 percent of Catholics who age 55 and over (See Figure 2.2).

Thus, there is good reason to believe that levels of Catholic involvement will decline further in the years ahead. Older Catholics with higher rates of involvement are being replaced by younger Catholics who do not attach as much importance to the Church, are more willing to leave the Church, do not attend Mass as often, donate less money to the Church, and read the Bible less often.

Of course, all other things are never equal. There are changes (e.g., population shifts) which can be anticipated and other events—such as councils of bishops and controversial encyclicals—which cannot be anticipated. These contextual factors also impinge on Catholics' involvement in the Church and modify cohort projections in one direction or the other. For example, to the extent that the percentage of Catholics in white-collar occupations increases—as it is expected to—the projected downturn in involvement may be moderated. However, to the extent that

Figure 2.2
Church Involvement of Three Age Groups
(Percents)

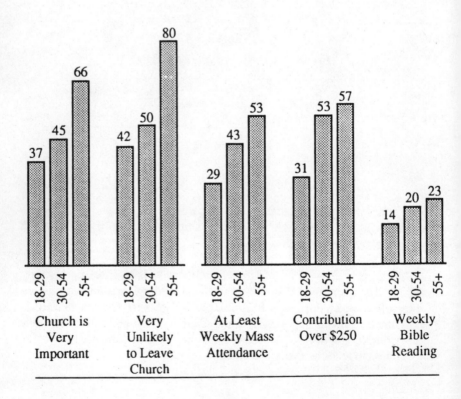

the expected increase in the percentage of Black, Hispanic, and single Catholics also occurs (and/or the Church doesn't become more attractive to members of these groupings), the downturn could be even sharper in the years ahead. Of course, we cannot take into account other unanticipated social or religious developments which also might affect our baseline projection. However, the more Church leaders do to foster involvement among young Catholics (e.g., increase their enrollment in Catholic schools), the more they can moderate our downward projections and increase overall rates of involvement in the years ahead.

Implications

Our data suggest there is great social diversity among Catholics and this diversity fosters variations in Catholics' involvement in the Church. The most important differences—with the most favorable contexts listed in parentheses—seem to be region of the country one lives in (Southwest), one's occupation (white collar), amount of Catholic schooling (more), and ethnicity (being Polish). Other factors which also make some difference include gender (being female), marital status (married), race (white), total education (more), and family income (high).

The data also indicate that rates of involvement in the Church vary a great deal over time. Recent fluctuations are related to social and religious changes which have taken place among Catholics over the last 25 to 30 years. In some respects, which we have emphasized in this chapter, these changes are quantitative: though rates of involvement remain relatively high, they have declined over the last two to three decades. In other respects, which have been mentioned here and will be stressed again in later chapters, these changes are qualitative in nature, having to do with changes in the meaning and expectations associated with older religious beliefs and practices (e.g., Mass attendance, confession, not eating meat on Fridays), the introduction of, or increased emphasis on, new ones (e.g., reading the Bible), and changes in the laity's conception of what it takes to be a "good Catholic" (see Chapter 3).

These findings have several implications for Catholic leaders. Diversity always has been a normal part of the Catholic experience, and it continues to be. This diversity was quite apparent to one of the writers when he recently attended a black Catholic Mass on the East Side of San Antonio (a Mass where the choir director appeared to be more important than the priest, and the music was based on black spirituals more than Gregorian Chant) and, one hour later, attended an Hispanic Mass on the West Side of the city (where Mariachi music and Spanish songs dominated the Mass). Other differences which we have noted—between men and women, married couples and single people, and laity with different amounts of Catholic schooling—also have deep historical roots and are highly institutionalized parts of our heritage.

Some of these differences may not be quite as salient as they have been in the past. For example, the cultural differences between European ethnic groups are diminishing somewhat with the Americanization process. But others—such as the differences between European, Hispanic, and Asian Catholics and among Asian American Catholics themselves—may be increasingly significant in the years ahead.

The positive features of these different experiences need to be appreciated and celebrated by all members of the Church. Religious leaders need to learn from the experiences of all groups, especially those which seem to generate the highest levels of involvement, to see what it is about their experiences which account for the importance they attach to the Church and their eagerness to support it. The lessons learned should then be examined to see if and how they might pertain to other groups or might be incorporated into the Church's social and educational programs. Church leaders also should explore ways of fostering a climate within the Church which encourages even greater involvement on the part of "marginalized" groups such as women, singles, and low income Catholics.

Change also has been an integral part of our experience There have been periods of increased interest in the Church, followed by periods of less fervor. During the pre-Vatican II period, American Catholics participated in many different liturgical and devotional activities such as Mass, novenas, and rosaries. In more recent years, the trend has been toward lower overall rates of involvement in such practices. And, according to the data in Table 2.5, this trend is likely to continue in the years ahead.

However, we caution against dramatic projections based solely on present circumstances. Those circumstances can change and are quite likely to do so. Some of the changes (e.g., increased migration to states such as Louisiana and Texas; increases in the percentage of Catholics in white-collar positions; and increased enrollments of Catholics in Catholic schools) probably would increase overall levels of involvement, while others (e.g., increases in the percentage of single and Hispanic Catholics) probably would lower overall rates of involvement.

In light of these negative projections and uncertain conditions, we think clergy and lay leaders ought to pay close attention to the laity's values and interests; look for ways in which lay people can express these concerns in all phases of Church life; and find ways in which clergy and lay people can share in the development of policies and programs related to these concerns. We turn our attention to the laity's image of who is a "good Catholic."

References

Davidson, James D., and Dean D. Knudsen. 1977. "A New Approach to Religious Involvement." *Sociological Focus* 10 (April): 251-273.

Davidson, James D., Dean D. Knudsen, and Stephen R. Lerch. 1983. "Involvement in Family, Religion, Education, Work, and Politics." *Sociological Focus* 16 (January): 13-36.

Gallup, George. 1985. *Religion in America: 50 Years (1935-1985)*. Princeton, NJ: The Gallup Report.

Greeley, Andrew M. 1977. *The American Catholic*. New York: Basic Books.

_____. 1986. *The Confessions of a Parish Priest*. New York: Pocket Books.

Greeley, Andrew M., and Peter H. Rossi. 1968. *The Education of Catholic Americans*. New York: Doubleday/Anchor Books.

3.

On Being a Good Catholic: Changing Definitions

Andrew Greeley has described Vatican II and its aftermath as a watershed experience for American Catholics. The aftermath, of course, included the discussion and debate that led up to and continued from Pope Paul VI's Encyclical *Humanae Vitae* (H.V.) in 1968 to Pope John Paul II's various declarations in defense of H.V. during the past few years. Indeed, if there is one thing both conservative Catholics and progressive Catholics agree on, it is that this has been a watershed experience. It has radically altered our idea of what it means to be a good Catholic.

In this chapter we review the changing meaning of the term "good Catholic" over the past 30 years, the most tumultuous generation in the past 100 years of the Church in American life. We will then proceed to consider some of the implications of this new meaning.

Before Vatican II it was easy to know who was a good Catholic, or at least what it took to be one. The formula was straightforward: study, learn and believe in the Baltimore Catechism, and accept the pope and his teachings as the unerring voice of God on earth. Of course there were lots of specific rules. A good Catholic was one who went to Mass every Sunday and holy day of obligation. Indeed, a good Catholic knew what those holy days were and when they occurred. A good Catholic went to confession about once or twice a month, usually before going to receive communion.

Good Catholics tipped their hats whenever they walked by the front of a Catholic Church, blessed themselves before kneeling and entering a church pew before Mass, contributed to the financial support of the parish, the diocese and Rome, and seldom complained in public about the official organization of the Church, sermons on money, or the sacrifices required of "this vale of tears." In fact, it was the stringent discipline of the Church that gave Catholicism its distinctive characteristic, that marked it as resistant to the hedonism of modern life.

It was not expected that good Catholics would never sin; on the contrary, as weak and frail humans, good Catholics were expected to sin occasionally. And to prepare good Catholics for those occasions, the Church helped him or her distinguish between venial (slight) sins and mortal (grave) sins. Confession was the mechanism by which Catholics cleansed themselves of their sins. Thus, the lines outside the confessional on a Saturday afternoon or evening were not so much signs of straying or bad Catholics as they were of good Catholics. In defense of this position, Varacalli (1987: 142) states the matter thus:

> One could argue, as most traditional Catholics do, that doctrine is central to Catholicism and that the institutional Church can and should be forgiving of human finitude and imperfection but it must also set doctrinal standards upon which moral practice can be judged. The Church, simply put, can forgive the sinner but never the sin.

A good Catholic would also remember not to eat meat on Friday or any of the other proscribed days of the year, and would store up indulgences against the time he or she might expect to spend in purgatory— good Catholics knew better than to expect to go directly to heaven when they died. Of course, good Catholics would never allow themselves to say the Protestant part of the Lord's Prayer, nor go into a Protestant church or Jewish synagogue, even to attend a wedding. And good Catholics sent their children to Catholic schools whenever possible.

A good Catholic who was also a woman had other identifiable characteristics: if she were unmarried, she would be like Mary, pure and undefiled; she could choose to be a bride of Christ by becoming a nun, or a wife to a husband to whom she owed loving obedience. For the good Catholic woman knew the meaning of St. Paul's famous words: "Man is the head of the woman as Christ is the head of the Church" (Ephesians 5:23). A leading Catholic marriage manual of the 1950s put the matter succinctly:

> In some cases the wife will have a powerful influence on her husband, which is as it should be. . . . The husband's position has significance mainly when some important decision has to be made (for example, a move to a new house) and there is no immediate agreement. If the decison cannot be postponed until there is harmony of viewpoint, then the responsibile husband will make the decision, and the loving wife will cheerfully acquiesce in the decision with humility. The husband, more than she, symbolizes law, authority, order, and any attempt to belittle him or deny his headship in such matters will certainly incur his wrath and destroy before the children the image of God's fatherhood that man was chosen to exemplify. (Kelly, 1958:7).

We take the time to quote this passage because it exemplifies the way Catholic men and women in the era before Vatican II were preached to, instructed in the ways of being good Catholics, and assured of what their true natures were by an unerring Church. After all, this marriage manual had an *imprimatur* and a *nihil obstat* from Francis Cardinal Spellman of New York, at that time the most influential churchman in the U.S.A.[1]

---

1. An *imprimatur* is the official right to publish a particular book and a *nihil obstat* means it is free of doctrinal or moral error. And a good Catholic knew the meaning of these Latin words and gave particular attention to books that had them, avoiding books on topics like marriage and family that did not have them.

The parish studies carried out by Fichter (1951; 1958) had shown that the image that the laity had of who was a good Catholic generally focused around such sacramental and liturgical matters as attending mass, confession, communion and the like.

Our study in 1987 attempts to measure just how much of a watershed experience the 1960s and their aftermath were in terms of the profile of the good Catholic that existed so firmly in just about everyone's mind in the days before Vatican II.

The Good Catholic

"The following statements deal with what you think it takes to be a good Catholic. Please tell me if you think a person can be a good Catholic without performing these actions?" The intent of the question was to ascertain the degree to which behaviors that were deemed essential characteristics of a good Catholic thirty years ago were still so considered.

Most of the items in the question deal with behavior having to do with liturgical and sacramental matters or with obedience to Church teachings. Only one involves a question of acceptance of a belief, in this case, the infallibility of the pope. The items are arranged in Table 3.1 in descending order of positive ("Yes") responses.

A majority of Catholics gave yes answers to seven of the ten items in the question, including all the liturgical and sacramental items. A generation ago it was a grave sin to miss Mass on Sunday without a good reason. Contemporary Catholics do not see that as an impediment to one's being a good Catholic, nor do they see the need for private confession or reception of communion during the Easter season. Perhaps the most reasonable explanation for this change lies in the decision of Vatican II to abandon formally the ban on meatless Fridays. Suddenly, what had been a grave sin all their lives was no longer so. They went on to ask, "If not meatless Fridays, then why Sunday Mass and other dis-

Table 3.1

Can A Person Be A Good Catholic Without Performing These Actions (Percent Saying "Yes")

Without going to Church every Sunday	70%
Without contributing money annually to the special collection for the pope (Peter's Pence)	68
Without obeying the Church's teaching regarding birth control	66
Without going to private confession at least once a year	58
Without obeying the Church's teaching regarding divorce and remarriage	57
Without receiving communion during the Easter time	54
Without getting married in the Church	51
Without believing in the infallibility of the pope	45
Without donating time or money to help the poor	44
Without obeying the Church's teaching regarding abortion	39

ciplines?" It is no wonder that conservatives see this new Catholicism as mushy and soft, no longer true to the stern discipline that was the pride of pre-Vatican II Catholicism.

In recent years general absolution given during the Mass itself has replaced the private confesial for many Catholics. Studies show that while less than 25% of Catholics now make use of the private confessional, a great majority of Catholics who do attend Mass receive communion. These changes concern conservatives. For example, in response to this change of behavior, Pope John Paul II(1988: C 10) stated recently that "the Sacrament of Penance is in crisis," and called upon the U.S. bishops "to restore the Sacrament of Penance to its rightful place in the Church," while at the same time warning against the growing practice of "general absolution."

In the late 1950s, about 75% of American Catholics said they had attended Mass in the previous week. By 1987, this figure had dropped to 52%. (See Figure 2.1, page 44). In our 1987 study, only 44% said they attended Mass at least weekly. Thus, while attendance at Mass has dropped dramatically in the past 30 years, the percentage of Mass attenders receiving communion has risen. Before Vatican II it was customary for Catholics to go to confession before receiving communion. The average Catholic went to confession and communion once or twice a month.

By 1980, only 12% of young Catholics (18-29) reported going to confession at least monthly, and even among the age group 50 and older, only 26% said they did (PRRC, 1980: 85). But two-thirds of churchgoers were receiving communion (Fee et al, 1981: 6). Clearly, more and more Catholics are saying that you can be a good Catholic and receive communion whenever you go to church without first going to private confession. It would seem that Catholics have become more sacramental in one area (communion) as they have decided that certain kinds of behavior are no longer sinful and/or require private sacramental confession.

A majority of respondents also believe a person can be a good Catholic who disobeys the Church's teaching on birth control, on divorce and remarriage, and even on getting married in the Church. Marriage in the Church is another discipline that lacks a firm theological base, as it is recognized that the couple marry each other and the priest and others merely serve as witnesses.

Birth control and remarriage after divorce have been among the most controversial doctrinal issues since Vatican II, with a significant number of clergy and bishops as well as theologians in disagreement with the traditional church teaching. We have already indicated in Chapter 1 the circumstances during the period 1960-65 that seem to have been most crucial in bringing about the change in the laity's beliefs about birth control. The divorce and remarriage issue has festered for more than a generation. It came to a head in the late 1960s in a period when all institutional practices were being challenged by one or another sector of the body politic. Between the late 1960s and 1970s a record number and percentage of Americans became divorced and remarried, and Catholics joined them in almost proportionate numbers (McCarthy, 1979).

Birth control and divorce/remarriage are matters of interpersonal relationships that most married couples and most family members have direct experience with. To the extent that couples think through the matter of whether and what contraceptives to use, and conclude that contraceptives other than rhythm are also legitimate and not sinful, they confront and challenge the teaching authority of the pope. We know that many Catholic couples used contraceptives other than rhythm in the past. The difference between then and now is that then they "knew" it was a sin. They either confessed the sin in order to receive forgiveness and then be in spiritual condition to receive communion, or in many cases, simply did not go to confession or communion.

Today, the majority of Catholics who use contraceptives do not believe they are sinning, and if they go to Mass, they receive communion. Thus, it is is not surprising that the great majority in our study say that you can be a good Catholic without obeying the Church's teaching on birth control.

On the question of papal infallibility, the respondents in the 1987 survey were split, with 45% saying you could be a good Catholic without believing that the pope was infallible when speaking out on matters of faith and morals, and 46% saying you could not. Since Vatican II, and especially since the proclamation of *Humanae Vitae,* significant numbers of Catholics have questioned the teaching on papal infallibility. It is possible that much of the loss of papal credibility can be traced to that encyclical, as people who disagreed with it came also to question the wisdom of the person who enunciated it (Greeley: 1979; 1977). It is important to remember, also, that so far no pope has declared the Church's teaching on birth control to be infallible. For that matter, neither are any of the other teachings on sexual conduct declared to be infallible.

On only two items did a majority say that a person could not be a good Catholic: 51% said a person could not be a good Catholic who did not donate time or money to help the poor, and 55% said the same about a person who did not obey the Church's teaching on abortion. Let us consider the latter item first.

Since the U.S. Supreme Court Decision in January 1973 outlawing all laws against abortion, there has been a gradual and increasingly effective campaign mounted to restrict and eventually overturn that decision. The campaign, which has become a nationwide social movement, has been spearheaded by Catholic laity and hierarchy. The issue reached a high point in 1984 when Cardinal O'Connor of New York led an attack on the Democratic vice-presidential candidate for her position in support of the right to abortion in a pluralistic society. He declared that a Catholic in good conscience could not vote for a Catholic who supported what he termed the Free Choice position. And when a group of Catholics signed a *New York Times* ad in support of the Free Choice position on abortion, the battle lines were drawn. In varying degrees, the Catholic hierarchy, led by the pope but with strong support from the U.S. Catholic Conference, has made abortion the litmus test of who is the good Catholic in these times.

On the one hand, our finding that 55% say that you cannot be a good Catholic without obeying the Church's teaching may be taken as evidence of the effectiveness of the Church's efforts to oppose abortion. At the same time, given the national effort that has been made by the "Right to Life" movement and the Church leadership, it is also noteworthy that 39% of those who called themselves Catholic said a person could be a good Catholic and still oppose the Church's teaching.

In a recent article in which he compared findings from the Notre Dame Parish Life Study and the Gallup Poll, Castelli (1987: 33-34), noted that among "churched" Catholics in the Parish Life Study, 69% found abortion acceptable in cases of rape and incest. An additional 6 % would accept abortion in most circumstances. In the Gallup survey, 79% said that abortion was acceptable in at least some circumstances. Thus, it would appear that Church leaders and "Right to Life" Catholics have had more success in making abortion the litmus test for who is a good Catholic than for creating and sustaining outright opposition to abortion.

A finding that may be related was that a majority (51%) also said you could not be a good Catholic if you did not help the poor. Taken in the context of the idea that life should be valued not only in the fetal stage but also once people are born into the world, this response seems consistent with that on abortion. But conservatives and liberals tend to diverge on this point. Conservatives tend to see the abortion question as separate and an absolute, while the question of helping the poor is more relative and often left to a matter of individual not collective action.

Factors Affecting Who Is Seen as a Good Catholic

In Table 3.2 we examine how the variables of age, education, income, Mass attendance and importance of the Church affect the five indicators of being a good Catholic that are concerned with sacramental and liturgical matters.

Several patterns are evident in the demographic data presented in Table 3.2. For the most part, they tell us what we should expect. Two somewhat distinctive profiles of American Catholics appear: those who are young, with higher incomes, some college education, who seldom or never go to Mass, and who say that the Church is not terribly important to them, contrast most sharply with older Catholics, those with lower incomes, less than a high-school education, who attend Mass regularly, and who say the Church is the most important or among the most important parts of their lives. This broad generalization needs qualification.

Table 3.2

Percentage of Catholics Who Say You Can Be A Good Catholic Without Obeying the Church's Teaching On—

		Sunday Mass	Confession	Communion	Marriage in Church	Giving to Peter's Pence
All:		70%	58%	54%	51%	68%
Age:	18-29	77	58	57	57	71
	30-39	74	66	64	56	73
	40-54	69	58	54	55	68
	55 & older	61	52	43	37	62
Education:						
Some high school		67	49	40	44	66
High school graduate		66	55	52	50	61
Some college		75	68	61	55	78
College graduate		78	66	66	56	79
Income:						
Under $10,000		69	56	36	44	65
$10,000-$19,999		59	47	49	51	67
$20,000-$29,999		72	67	56	57	71
$30,000-$39,999		66	55	56	51	56
$40,000+		77	65	67	59	80
Mass Attendance:						
At least weekly		53	52	43	44	63
At least monthly		83	56	56	49	65
Seldom or never		88	73	70	68	81
Importance of Church:						
Most important		51	45	38	36	55
Among most important		64	54	44	42	64
Quite important		78	62	62	59	73
Not terr. important		90	77	75	67	85

Not all young people are college-educated, earn high incomes, and sel-dom if ever attend Mass or say the Church is not terribly important to them. Nor are all those over age 45 traditional in their view of who is a good Catholic. Several relationships between social location and religious attitudes are evident in the Table.

1. Age is inversely related to liberal attitudes; older people are more likely than the younger to hold traditional attitudes about who is a good Catholic. As we will see throughout this book, Catholics over age 55 are consistently the most traditional.

2. Education is directly correlated with liberal attitudes. Those with at least some college education were significantly more liberal on three of the five items, and in all cases expressed the more liberal attitudes.

3. Income is directly related to liberal attitudes about who is a good Catholic; the higher the level of income, the more liberal is the attitude. This pattern held on all five items.

4. The two measures of commitment to the Catholic Church , Mass attendance and importance of the Church to the individual were inversely related to liberal attitudes; those who go to Mass at least weekly and who say the Catholic Church is the most important or among the most important parts of their lives were significantly more likely to support traditional attitudes than those who seldom go to Mass or who say that the Church is not terribly important to them. Thus, the two commitment variables were the most predictive of support for the traditional image of who is a good Catholic.

In Table 3.3 we see the same patterns repeated for the items dealing with personal moral conduct like birth control and abortion, and for the one item having to do with a belief, namely, the infallibility of the pope. In some cases, the differences are even more sharply defined than in the previous Table, for example, with regard to birth control, remarriage after divorce, and abortion.

Other generalizations evident in these two tables are also noteworthy. For example, on some issues like going to Church every Sunday, even among those who are regular church attenders, a majority support the

Table 3.3

Percentage Saying You Can Be A Good Catholic Without Obeying Church's Teaching On—

		Birth Control	Divorce/ Remarriage	Abortion	Helping Poor	Papal Infallibility
All:		66%	57%	39%	44%	45%
Age:	18-29	75	63	44	45	46
	30-39	76	68	48	45	52
	40-54	67	60	41	42	49
	55 & older	48	39	25	44	37
Education:						
Some high school		53	47	32	48	41
High school graduate		62	55	38	43	41
Some college		73	63	44	46	49
College graduate		82	68	45	41	55
Income:						
Under $10,000		51	49	29	48	36
$10,000-$19,999		53	56	37	50	43
$20,000-$29,999		71	56	37	50	43
$30,000-$39,999		76	60	43	40	41
$40,000 +		77	69	47	44	53
Mass Attendance:						
At least weekly		54	45	26	41	35
At least monthly		73	63	43	41	46
Seldom or never		79	74	59	54	63
Importance of Church:						
Most important		30	25	17	38	33
Among most important		61	50	29	44	34
Quite important		78	67	49	44	51
Not terr. important		86	84	64	49	72

liberal position that you don't have to obey the traditional teaching to be a good Catholic.

For the most part, Catholics over age 55 accept the Church's teaching that only rhythm is an acceptable form of birth control. Studies as late as the early 1960s showed that a majority of all Catholics accepted the Church's teachings on matters such as birth control and abortion. The implications from our data are that the older Catholics continue to adhere to the traditional position more than any other age group. Meanwhile, the baby boomers, those between the ages of 30 and 39, consistently show themselves to be at the most liberal end of the spectrum, along with the youngest age group, for whom Vatican II and the birth-control debates of the 1960s are vaguely known, historical events.

Most studies of age cohorts and aging show that people do not necessarily become more conservative as they age (Riley, 1987: 1-14). For example, cohorts develop a kind of group consciousness based on the particular socialization processes that accompany them through the historical events that mark their era. Different historical events of different eras shape people for life. Thus, the events that shaped the lives of the baby boomers in their youth are expected to work themselves out in the context of the "aging effect" with a continuing liberal tone. And that in turn means less support for the traditional image of who is a good Catholic.

Given the fact that over the past 30 years the income and education levels of Catholics in the United States have risen dramatically, and that both higher education and higher income are predictors of liberal positions on moral questions such as birth control, divorce and remarriage, our data also strongly suggest that the definition of who is a good Catholic is likely to continue to undergo change away from the traditional sacramental and liturgical patterns, that is, confession, Mass attendance and the like.

Men, Women and the Good Catholic

We tested to see whether gender would be a predictor of attitudes, beliefs and moral prescriptions. On six of the ten items it was not. On seven of the ten items, majorities of men and women (ranging from 54% on marriage in church to 92% regarding birth control), supported the statement that you could be a good Catholic without obeying the traditional teaching. Men and women differed significantly on the following items:

Table 3.4

Percent Saying You Can Be A Good Catholic Without—

	Men	Women
Obeying the Church on abortion	54	41
Helping the poor	34	54
Believing in infallibility of Pope	63	49
Giving to Peter's Pence	65	87

The only item on which less than a majority of the men (34%) say you can be a good Catholic is on helping the poor. It is difficult to interpret this finding. Perhaps men, who are still more likely to be major breadwinners than are women in Catholic families, feel it is a duty to contribute to the material welfare of others, while women, a significant proportion of whom did not work for wages outside the home, were less sensitive to this question.

Women were much more traditional on the abortion and papal infallibility questions, which, given that larger numbers were older and less well-educated, seems to make sense. And while both took the same position on giving to Peter's Pence, the women were significantly more likely to do so, which seems to follow the logic of their response on giving to help the poor.

Discussion and Conclusion

We have found that the definition of who is a good Catholic has undergone a radical transformation from what it was at the beginning of this century. The definition has changed and continues to change not because Church leaders have sought the change, but because of factors operating in the larger society that have influenced the Church and helped bring about Vatican II. In part, they constitute "the signs of the times" that Pope John XXIII alluded to when he called for Vatican II. The Church in the United States has become an integral part of American society even as it continues to be part of the Universal Church headquartered in the Vatican. As we have indicated in Chapter 1, the laity have been greatly influenced by the democratic, individualistic, freedom-oriented ethos of American society.

Certainly the changing definition of who is or can be a good Catholic owes much not only to American society but to Vatican II and the changes it implemented. The most important change it legitimated for Catholics worldwide was the acknowledgement of the right of individual conscience, the right, indeed the obligation, of the individual to think issues through and make her or his own moral judgments, aided by Church teachings. One result is that traditional sacramental and liturgical practices are no longer seen as defining who is a good Catholic.

Conservatives, of course, challenge this interpretation of Vatican II and the findings of studies like ours. Speaking directly to Greeley's work—but he might as well have been speaking to these findings—one conservative says:

> Greeley, thus, speaks of the "anguish" that American Catholic laity went through during the sixties and seventies over the Church's position on sexual and marital relations. He assumes honest, soul-searching, prayerful and legitimate dissent. It never occurs to him that some, if not much , of this "dissent" was taken because it was the easy way out; that it was as much the result of selfishness and

convenience as anything else. Or, in other cases, that "dissent" simply reflects a profound ignorance of, and lack of acculturation into, the tenets of the Catholic faith. Greeley, in short, would profit by an honest reading of *The Ratzinger Report,* which lays out almost diametrically opposed assumptions regarding the individual, culture and society, and the nature of the Church. (Varacalli,1987: p. 141)

Varacalli may have a point, but it would be the same point that can be made about the commitment that many if not most conservatives have toward the Church, namely that it reflects chance (being born Catholic), convenience, and blind obedience without any deep understanding of the tenets of the faith or the nature of the individual, culture and society. He would be on more solid ground were he to focus attention on the way that the broad secular culture has always impacted religious organizations, even as the latter have influenced the culture of the larger society.

In the light of Vatican II and the momentous events in American society that have occured before, during and after Vatican II, the changing definition of a good Catholic seems most likely to reflect the times. Let us review the findings:

1. There is consensus across all groups that you can be a good Catholic without going to Mass at least once a week. While Sunday Mass was a strictly enforced discipline until Vatican II, it has just about disappeared as a matter of disciplinary concern since Vatican II. Elders as well as youngsters, with whatever level of formal education and income, can appreciate this relaxation of discipline, especially as Sunday the day of rest has been replaced by Sunday the day for shopping, recreation and work. Many Catholics now attend Mass Saturday afternoon or evening as an alternative to Sunday. Church leaders seem satisfied with this accomodation. But this relaxation of time has not brought the percentages back to the pre-Vatican II levels; at best, it has helped stem the tide.

2. Contributing to Peter's Pence is also seen as a matter of personal choice, without any apparent moral obligation attached to it. And there is overwhelming consensus that one can be a good Catholic without contributing, again, regardless of age, education, income level, frequency of Mass attendance, or importance of the Church to the individual.

3. Three questions dealing with matters of marriage and sexuality have been among the most controversial in the past 30 years: birth control, divorce and remarriage, and abortion. And here Church leaders and laity have been in increasing disagreement. We need not repeat the basic concerns here. Rather, the important finding and implication is that the laity continue to dissent from the fundamental teachings while insisting that they can still be good Catholics in the process. The data strongly suggest that the closer the behavior (use of contraceptives, getting a divorce and then remarrying without Church permission, and having or advocating an abortion) to the real-life experience of the individual or some family member or friend, the more likely is the individual to dissent from the traditional teaching. And to the extent that people don't see the behavior as sinful, it follows that they believe one can be a good Catholic and still not obey the Church's teaching. Abortion is the least likely to gain broad support, with only the seldom or never Mass attenders and those who say the Church is not terribly important in the majority on this issue. But even among those who attend Mass at least weekly, one in four say it is possible to dissent and still be a good Catholic.

4. The changing behavior regarding confession and communion are an outgrowth of Vatican II. It may well be that as Fr. Ives Congar stated, sexual behavior was the main reason why so many people went to confession, and/or did not receive communion regularly. With the birth control issue resolved so far as the laity are concerned, the need for confession before communion would have greatly diminished. Besides, many of the laity now understand that they receive general absolution during the prayers at the beginning of the Mass. And given the fact that Americans have not been socialized to see themselves as guilty of such sins as pride, gluttony, envy, covetousness, to name a few possible "other

grave" sins, it is not surprising that there is simply much less to confess. Thus, the data give little encouragement to those who would support Pope John Paul II's plea for a return to the private confessional.

5. With regard to helping the poor, the only group with a majority saying you could be a good Catholic and not help was the seldom/never Mass attenders. We will examine the question about helping the poor in more detail in a later chapter when we consider the recent pastorals of the U.S. bishops on nuclear war and the economy. Suffice to note here that the laity are more likely to question the quality of a person's Catholicism if they don't help the poor than if they don't go to Mass on Sunday, or if they use contraceptives other than rhythm. This is further evidence that they seem to be giving more heed to the social gospel than to the traditional practices of the institutional Church.

6. The Catholic laity's obligation to believe in the infallibility of the pope when he speaks on matters of faith and morals is not widely seen as crucial. Younger people, college graduates, the seldom Mass attenders and those who did not see the Church as terribly important to them, each had a majority saying that you could be a good Catholic without believing in the pope's infallibility. If these people continue to identify themselves as Catholic, given their growing proportion of the total Catholic population in the United States, they can be expected to continue to challenge and question official Church teachings, even if the pope should declare them infallible.

Conservatives like Varacalli would probably welcome a move on the part of the church hierarchy to demand orthodoxy, arguing that while there would be significant losses in membership initially, in the long run the Church would be purified. And, a distinctive orthodox Catholicism would be as likely to attract new members as have the Mormons, evangelical Protestants and orthodox Jews. Or, perhaps, the Church would then more closely resemble the Church in western European countries.

Varacalli (1987: 160) reminds us that while the fundamentalist churches have all been growing, the liberal and progressive churches have been shrinking in numbers.

Were such an event as excommunication for those who refuse to acknowledge the sinfulness of contraceptive birth control and remarriage after divorce to occur, the trauma would be maximized. It seems improbable to expect a majority of Catholics now practicing contraceptive birth control to cease and accept the authority of the pope, unless and until a contraceptive acceptable to the papacy and to the great majority of couples is developed. Nor is it realistic to expect them to accept the practice of contraception as a sin to be confessed. Of course, the claim to infallibility may simply be ignored in the specific case by the laity, just as it is now questioned by almost half of them. It is not at all clear how a demand for orthodoxy would or could be carried out in such a mobile society. Besides, the sanction of excommunication is only meaningful if the people are somehow hurt by it, or fear it to such an extent that they will conform in order to avoid even the threat. It is questionable who would be hurt the most by a move that would leave the U.S. Church looking more and more like its western European counterparts.

Points of Comparison

In their study of Catholic Parish Life in the United States, Leege and his associates(1988) asked somewhat overlapping questions about "Who is a true Catholic." They relied entirely on behavioral measures, justify-

---

Percent Saying Persons Can Be Considered True Catholics Who—

1. Rarely go to Mass	50%
2. Are married outside the Church	55%
3. Urge or undergo abortion	25%

ing their decision on the grounds of "the American cultural propensity to judge people by what they do rather than by the hidden beliefs they hold . . ." Three of their behavioral measures are close enough to three of ours to merit a comparison here.

As seen in Table 3.1, in all three related cases, the national sample in our study was more liberal than the parish study sample, but the ordering of the items was the same, with the question on abortion receiving the least positive response in both cases.

Leege found that the strongest predictors of attitudes about who was a true Catholic were to be found in the people's orientation (traditional or liberal) toward the Church. Those who were the most traditional were the most restrictive, while those most open to change in the Church were the most liberal. Our measures of traditional orientation were Mass attendance and importance of the Church to them, and these were the most predictive of restrictive attitudes in our study. Thus, while the samples and the methodologies differ greatly, there is support for our findings in the Notre Dame Parish Studies.

One final note: the variable most predictive of support for the traditional Church image of who is a good Catholic is the one that measured the person's self-assessment of the importance of the Church to his or her life. Thirteen percent of the respondents in our survey said the Church was the most important feature of their lives. On seven of the ten items, less than 40% of these respondents said you could be a good Catholic and not adhere to traditional practices. And on only two items (Sunday Mass—51%, and Peter's Pence—55%) did even a small majority support a non-traditional stance. The downside of this finding, of course, is that only 13% of the respondents in our survey expressed this highest level of commitment. This is the same percentage as those who said the Church was not a terribly important part of their lives.

The overwhelming portion of the Catholic population in our study was in the middle categories; for them, the Church is important, but so are other parts of their lives. They also go to Mass almost every week.

They support the traditional image of the good Catholic most strongly on the issues of abortion, helping the poor, and papal infallibility. Since those respondents also tend to be among the older Catholics, their numbers are more likely to decrease than increase in the years ahead. Thus,it is hard to find any signs of the times that would lead us to expect a revival of the traditional image of the good Catholic.

These data support Greeley's findings of an emerging communal-type Catholic, only loosely tied to the institutional Church, who puts more and more emphasis on her/his own life experience. We turn now to Chapter 4 for further evidence on this newly emerging Catholic.

References

Castelli, James. 1987. "A Tale of Two Cultures." *Notre Dame Magazine*, Summer, pp. 33-34.

Fee, Joan L. , Andrew M. Greeley, William C. McCready, and Teresa A. Sullivan. 1980. *Young Catholics: A Report to the Knights of Columbus.* New York: Sadlier, p. 256.

Fichter, Joseph H. 1951. *The Dynamics of a City Parish.* Chicago: University of Chicago Press.

_____. 1958. *Parochial School: A Sociological Study.* Notre Dame: University of Notre Dame Press.

Kelly, George A. 1958. *The Catholic Marriage Manual.* New York: Random House.

Greeley, Andrew M. 1979. *Crisis in the Church.* Chicago: The Thomas More Association.

_____. 1977. *The American Catholic.* New York: Basic Books.

Leege, David C. 1988. "Who is a True Catholic? Social Boundaries on the Church." Report No. 12, March. *Notre Dame Study of Catholic Parish Life,* 1201 Memorial Library, Notre Dame, IN 46556.

Luker, Kristin. 1984. *Abortion and the Politics of Motherhood.* Berkeley: University of California Press.

McCarthy, John. 1979. "Religious Commitment, Affiliation and Marriage Dissolution," in Robert Wuthnow (ed.), *The Religious Dimension.* New York: Academic Press.

Paul VI, Pope. 1968. *Humanae Vitae, The Papal Encyclical on Birth Control.* Vatican City.

Princeton Religion Research Center (PRRC). 1980. *Religion in America, 1979-80.* Princeton, NJ.

Riley, Matilda White. 1987. "On the Significance of Age in Sociology." *American Sociological Review* 52: 1-14.

Varacalli, Joseph A. 1987. "The State of the American Catholic Laity: Propositions and Proposals." *Faith and Reason,* pp. 126-166.

John Paul II, Pope. 1988. *Washington Post.* "Pope Urges Bishops to Encourage Confession." Section C10, June 4.

4.

How Strong Is the Church's Moral Authority?

We begin with a recent event which exemplifies key issues in moral authority. On January 22, 1986, Mrs. Mary Ann Sorrentino, the Catholic executive director of Planned Parenthood of Rhode Island, disclosed to the press that she had been excommunicated a half year earlier by the diocesan chancery, due to her leadership of an agency which helps women get abortions. She explained that she hadn't told anyone earlier, to avoid publicity. But now the fact had been revealed in a TV show, so she was talking to the media about it.

She had been in her job for nine years, and no action had been taken against her by the Catholic Church until the previous spring, when her 15-year-old daughter had been preparing for confirmation. The local priest singled out the daughter for a personal discussion about abortion (which Mrs. Sorrentino and her husband attended), and the priest directly asked the girl whether she would ever have an abortion. She said no, though she defended the right of others to do so. This satisfied the priest, and the daughter was confirmed. The priest said to Mrs. Sorrentino that she was excommunicated, and a few days later a letter arrived confirming it.

Of course she was angry. But she decided to remain in her job and maintain her beliefs regarding abortion without any change. She would continue going to church, praying, and being a moral Christian. She raised questions about why she was singled out, when many other Catholics were helping women get abortions and even helping perform them; why weren't they excommunicated? She asked why her daughter had been called in for a special talk with the priest. But these were secondary justifications for her behavior; the main one was that she said her informed conscience was her final authority in women's reproductive matters, above the Church or the Pope. The church leaders lacked credibility because they had too little close knowledge of the issues and were often insensitive to women. She did not accept their authority on this question. And she did not back down.

The chancery official did not back down either. He simply quoted Canon Law which says that anyone assisting another person in getting an abortion is to be excommunicated.[1] There is no requirement of an edict by a bishop or a hearing for the person excommunicated. He had simply followed church authority (see *Providence Journal,* 23 January 1986, p. A6; *New York Times,* 25 January 1986). Mrs. Sorrentino too had invoked authority—her prayers to God about the issues and her well-informed conscience. Both claimed authority for their actions.

Measuring Authority

The concept "authority" is used not only in religion but also in government and science. Social scientists have defined it as a relationship between people in which one trusts and follows another. In Max Weber's classic definition, authority is "the probability that certain

---

1. The new Code of Canon Law (Canon Law Society, 1983) states that a person incurs automatic excommunication for any of seven acts: helping someone get a completed abortion; a physical attack on the Pope; breaking the seal of confession (that is, divulging what has been told a priest in confession); granting absolution to an accomplice in a crime; illicit ordination of a bishop; desecration of the Holy Eucharist; and defiant heresy (Canons 1364, 1367, 1360, 1378, 1383, 1388, 1398).

specific commands from a given source will be obeyed by a given group of persons" (Weber, 1947:324). This definition is usually adopted by analysts (e.g., Lasswell and Kaplan, 1950; Nisbet, 1966).

The main point here is that authority is not merely a proclamation by a leader, but also the probability that a follower will accept the claim and obey. Authority must be analyzed at two levels, sometimes called *claimed authority* (or formal authority) and *accepted authority*; the former is the claim of the would-be leader and the latter is the actual empirical level of acceptance of the claim by followers. Accepted authority is a matter in the hands of the followers, who make decisions based on their perceptions of the leader and the leader's justification for the authority claims.

Normally there is a gap between claimed authority and accepted authority; more is claimed than is actually accepted. This is very common in social behavior, when some groups of followers doubt if the authority is warranted or if specific commands actually follow properly from basic principles. To analyze claimed authority one must look at the bases of moral claims, usually found in religious texts or political documents. Searching them out and explicating them is the work of theologians and philosophers. By contrast, to analyze accepted authority requires empirical measures of the degree to which followers accept the authority in word or deed. The survey discussed in this book is a good example. Claimed and accepted authority are never the same; a gap between them is common in human history, and in any situation researchers must investigate its depth, extent, and reasons.

Mary Ann Sorrentino did not reject most of the Church's authority claims. She did not rebel, for example, against church teachings about revelation, or sacraments, or the Trinity—only against the teachings on abortion. As for her reasons, she cited a lack of faith in the Vatican committees who framed the teachings on abortion, since other claims for authority and her other experiences had led her to conclusions which were different.

Authority is sustained only when the leader and followers both exist in a community of shared values and understandings. Only then can "legitimacy" (the belief by followers that a claim is proper and binding) develop, since it requires common grounds for authority claims. Leaders must appeal to the grounds of their authority to make their claims effective. Max Weber identified three "bases" of authority in human history. One is rational-legal authority, grounded in commonly-accepted constitutions or legal traditions; the second is charismatic authority, grounded in the personal forcefulness of the leader; and the third is traditional authority, based on age-old tribal or traditional ways of doing things (Weber, 1947:Book III). In the case of the Catholic Church, the grounds are clear—Christ's establishment of the Church in the New Testament and the centuries of tradition. In a strong and stable authority relationship, the leader need not justify each and every statement by referring to the common grounds, but he or she needs to keep the followers convinced that it can always be done if needed. Komonchak describes the situation:

> It is a sign of a serious problem in the social relationship if every act of A (the leader) is skeptically questioned by B (the follower). A 'credibility gap' is a crisis of authority. On the other hand, a consistent unwillingness of A to provide the reasons behind A's decisions is likely to generate the suspicion that no such reasons exist and to weaken B's constitutive acknowledgement of A's authority (1987:104).

Authority may reside in a person or in an institution. In a stable society there are several roles designated as having authority (judge, sheriff, executive, and so on) in the sense that they are trusted by most members of society as being responsible, capable, and just. The incumbents of these roles then enjoy authority from the office itself, which is different from authority earned from their own personal actions. The former is called "authority of office," and the latter "personal authority." Most leaders strive to strengthen both.

Lastly, authority always has a definite scope. Each authority claim is defined according to the topics covered and not covered. A scholar may claim to be an authority on modern European history or only on the World War II period. Similarly the scholar's accepted authority, in the view of the general public, may be broad or narrow, depending on the scholar's work and actions. A religious leader may claim broad moral authority or may renounce some areas of life (such as politics) and make a narrower claim—which may in turn be broadly or narrowly accepted by his or her followers.

The Moral Authority of the Catholic Church

Authority claimed by the Roman Catholic Church extends far beyond the realm of morals, but our interest here is limited to morals, the focus of greatest public attention in recent years. The accepted authority of the Church in moral decision-making, especially on the topic of sexuality and marriage, seems to be weakening. The credibility gap is described by observers as ominously great (as discussed in Chapter 1), causing weakened authority of church teachings on other topics as well. All during the 1970s and 1980s, research studies have shown a crisis of church authority regarding birth control, divorce, and related matters. For example, in 1963 over half of American Catholics accepted the Church's teaching that birth control was wrong, but twenty-four years later a 1987 poll reported that only 18 percent said it was sinful. Also, 52 percent approved of remarriage after divorce in 1963, but 73 percent did so in 1974 (Greeley, et al., 1976:35; *Los Angeles Times,* 1987; also see Gallup and Castelli, 1987).

Why has a large gap arisen? Are Catholics turning to alternative bases of moral authority in place of the Church's teachings? Are they being influenced by cultural shifts so that their very definition of authority has changed? Are they rebelling against the Church's traditional moral leadership? Observers have suggested all of these possibilities. The explanation most plausible to us is that two cultural currents have influenced Catholics in modern Western nations in their approach to church authority, and American Catholics have felt their force.

The first current is the experience of democracy and participation in political life. The doctrines of separation of powers and freedom of expression in the United States Constitution and Bill of Rights imply that no single person or institution can be trusted to have final truth in human questions—including religious and moral questions. Therefore a modern individual should not fully accept claims of authority by *anyone*. Governments should uphold political *processes,* but not particular moral judgments—which are assumed to change from time to time and from group to group. In the United States, citizens become accustomed to participatory structures in all institutions traditionally claiming authority; they take part in electoral politics, voluntary associations of all kinds, scientific debates, legal debates, juries, and even public policy commissions.

All of this feels normal and proper. Americans participate in elections at all levels, from local horticulture club to national president, and they are accustomed to constitutions at all levels designating terms of office and scope of leaders' power. No one seriously disputes that this is the best way of managing claims to authority. Protestant churches in the same communities use similar procedures. An implication is present here but seldom voiced: accepted authority can be achieved only through rational persuasion and demonstrated leadership, not through anyone's claim to superior truth or through coercion. Even more: no claim to truth is infallible or beyond dispute, and anyone who makes such a claim cannot expect to find many believers. This cultural setting creates a problem for the Catholic Church in its habitual claims for authority, not because of the content of its teachings but solely because modern people have learned to take a reserved posture toward *all* institutions claiming authority. The acids of modernity eat away at the claims of all.

The second cultural current is not from democratic experiences directly but from rising levels of education, especially in the social sciences and humanities. American Catholics are enrolling in college in ever-increasing numbers, and inevitably they are exposed to more and more nontraditional interpretations of society and history. The burgeoning behavioral sciences have explored the development of human intelligence, cultural relativity, sexuality and gender, genetics, and other topics hitherto studied only by philosophers and theologians. In Latin America a theology of liberation has arisen which is based partly on Marxist analyses of economics and politics. In Europe and the United States the understanding of human personality has been revolutionized by the Freudian revolution in the past half century. Today in America there is evidence of a rise of a "therapeutic ethic" as a guide to life (Rieff, 1966; Bellah, et al., 1985). One thrust common to all of these new scientific developments has been an increase in perceived possibilities in human life.

Because of the growth of behavioral science in this century, one might expect a larger crisis of church authority on the topics studied by behavioral scientists than on others, and these would certainly include sexuality, gender, and the whole range of physical and psychological therapies. Archbishop Weakland of Milwaukee states this argument clearly:

> Today's challenges to the Church come mostly from psychology and the human sciences. In fact, it is not by accident that the troubled territory today is sexuality and its relationship to the whole of human behavior, that is, moral issues (in Neuhaus, 1987:128).

The precise source and topography of the Church's authority problem today is difficult to know. Sociologists trying to dissect competing explanations are hampered, since too much has been happening at once, and data for describing historical trends is scarce. Most likely the correct explanation is broad in scope, not narrow, and not confined to problems with church teachings on sexuality and personal behavior. Probably these battles occur because of deeper underlying shifts, almost like underlying continental drift. Archbishop Weakland has recently said that the Church in the United States must come to terms with two critical contemporary questions: "(1) how its clergy—and especially its bishops—will relate as teachers to its highly intelligent and trained laity, and (2) how the Church as a whole will enter into the debate in American society on political, social, and economic issues" (1986:201). Let us look at the views of American Catholics in 1987.

Moral Authority on Sex and Marriage Issues

When designing the 1987 survey, we decided to focus primary attention on matters relating to sex and marriage. This does not imply that other moral issues are less important, but interview time was limited, and these issues are the subject of heated debate today.

In the interview we put six questions to the respondents, asking where ultimate moral authority regarding six issues *should* reside. Here is the exact wording:

Next, I would like your opinion on several issues that involve moral authority in the Catholic Church. In each case I would like to know who you think should have the final say about what is right or wrong. The choices are: A. The church leaders—the pope and bishops; B. Individuals taking church teachings into account and deciding for themselves; or C. Individuals and leaders working together.

These three options require some explaining. We did not put them into final form until we had done two waves of pretests, and the pretests taught us some important lessons.

Option A seems quite clear, and option B seems moderately clear. B states that final moral authority rests with the individual Catholic after taking church teachings into account. The implication is that the individual is, in the normal case, deciding a specific case involving himself or herself, not making public decisions or policies about moral questions. The implication is also that the individual in question is not responsible for others or for a group's collective action. The final wording was chosen because it seemed clear and natural to representative American Catholics on the telephone, and because we were asking about sex and marriage issues, which are often personal and private.

Option C is not quite so clear, since it does not specify how individuals and leaders should work together. It implies that individuals and leaders should cooperate in formulating *general* social teachings, but not in deciding specific cases. (In this way it calls for the influence of the *sensus fidelium*—the common consent of the faithful.) To us it is difficult to see how individuals and leaders working together could decide specific cases in a way different from those described in options A and B. In the end, someone needs to decide the concrete cases.

We included option C in the responses because some people in the pretests asked for it. Option C was their actual viewpoint, they told us; leaders and individuals must somehow work together in a true participative fashion to decide church teachings, and this working-together is the solution to the authority problem. The survey, therefore, needed such an option, even though it is not articulate as regards how it would be implemented. We included the option, since the primary aim of our research was to describe the current state of Catholic attitudes. Many Catholics really hope for future collaboration between church leaders and laity in discerning guidelines for moral behavior.

Before we look at the results, we need to clarify the church hierarchy's teachings on this question. Does Catholic teaching support A, B, or C, and has the teaching changed recently? We consulted with theological advisors, and they agreed that official Catholic teaching most supports option B. Furthermore, it has not changed for centuries. Ever since the Church's adoption of Thomas Aquinas's theology, it has held to Thomas's teaching that the well-formed individual conscience is the final moral authority. St. Thomas and his followers discussed in detail how the earnestness and faithfulness of the individual conscience might be assessed, and they stressed that church teachings are always to be taken as guidance, but in the end the individual must decide. Nothing during the Second Vatican Council or since changed that.

But the emphasis of teaching at the parish level has changed. The popular interpretation commonly given by priests has been modified since the 1960s, partly in response to the Council. We can understand this if we look back a little farther in history. After the Modernist controversies of 1900-1910, American Catholic seminaries became cautious and taught a doctrine of authority which was hierarchical and centralist. Moral theology manuals used in seminary teaching put greatest stress on the conformity of an individual's objective acts with church teaching as the criterion of sinfulness; the stress was on the authority of the official teaching (see Komonchak, 1982:71ff; Curran, 1985:225ff). In effect, the theology taught at the popular level resembled our option A, in that church teachings were put above individual consciences. The conservative theological climate of the worldwide Catholic Church promoted this tendency. Therefore, bishops and priests in American Catholicism from that time until the 1960s taught the faithful that final moral authority rested with church teachings—without explaining Thomas's doctrine of the role of the informed conscience.

Several important distinctions *were* made, and they affected practical church actions. Moral behavior in the public arena was always more sensitive and more carefully monitored than behavior in the private arena, since the former carries implications for the trust and devotion of the faithful. And moral statements concerning general principles were more circumscribed than statements on particular cases concerning particular people. Seminarians were told that in public one must always stress the official teachings of the Church, not the rights of individuals in particular situations—that is a matter for one-on-one counseling, not for homilies or catechetical lessons. In most cases the particular relationship of church teachings to conscience was left unclear, with the general thrust that church teachings are foremost.

Only with the experiences of the 1960s, including Vatican Council II and the *Humanae Vitae* controversy, was the emphasis on church teachings constrained and the importance of the well-informed individual conscience gradually explained and affirmed. Many seminaries and parishes articulated their teachings about moral decisions, giving more attention to the role of conscience (see Hennesey, 1981:327ff). But not all did so, resulting in much unevenness in teachings from diocese to diocese and from parish to parish. The new emphasis has provoked endless discussion, even puzzlement, among lay Catholics about how things have changed in the moral teaching department. Many Catholics born in

Table 4.1
Who Should Have The Final Say About Right Or Wrong?
(Percents)

	A. Church Leaders	B. Individuals	C. Both	D. Don't Know
Sexual relations outside of marriage	34	42	21	4
A Catholic who engages in homosexual behavior	32	39	19	10
Test-tube babies	30	37	25	8
A Catholic advocating free choice regarding abortion	29	45	22	4
A divorced Catholic remarrying without getting an annulment	23	31	43	4
A Catholic practicing contraceptive birth control	12	62	23	3

the 1910s, 1920s, or 1930s personally experienced the new emphasis on individual conscience, and even today they are working through its implications. No wonder people feel confused! Numerous lay persons told us of their dismay and concluded that "it all depends on which priest you talk to."

Let us see what the attitudes are today. (See Table 4.1.) The six questions are listed in order, based on the percentage of respondents choosing option A. (In the actual interview the order was different.) The issue on which the respondents most often saw final moral authority as properly remaining with church teachings is "sexual relations outside of marriage." Second is homosexual behavior. At the other extreme, one of the six is much lower than the others: "a Catholic practicing contraceptive birth control." Only 12 percent thought final authority on this question should rest with church teachings, while 62 percent said it should be with individuals.

The fourth issue in the table is that of "a Catholic advocating free choice regarding abortion." It is on freedom of advocacy in the Catholic community, not on abortion as such. The issue of abortion is so complex that we could not study it adequately in the constraints of this survey, so we opted to ask about freedom of *advocacy*, not abortion itself.

The main message from Table 4.1 is that most Catholics see final moral authority as properly residing *with the individual or with a process involving both church leaders and individuals.* The proportion accepting binding authority from the institutional church alone is small, never more than 34 percent.

To be clear, let us repeat that the issue is not whether the Christian individual is free to act following his or her moral decision. Of course he or she is free in the governmental sense; no church official can have him or her arrested or silenced. Rather, the issue is whether an action contrary to official church teachings, taken with full awareness of those teachings and all other considerations, can be affirmed as moral and sinless.

The official church teaching on the locus of authority is described by Komonchak, utilizing a distinction between "extraordinary" and "ordinary" teaching offices of the Pope, a distinction first made in the 19th century. The first refers to the limited number of teachings deemed to be infallible, and the second to all other papal teachings such as day-to-day sermons, addresses, and encyclicals. For the last century it has been taught that the faithful must give assent to extraordinary teachings, but with regard to the ordinary teachings the faithful must give respect to their authority and handle them with reverence. There is no requirement that the faithful must give assent and obedience to the ordinary (noninfallible) papal teachings if there are sufficient reasons for not doing so (Komonchak, 1982:77). This is similar to the teaching since St. Thomas, even though the special case of "extraordinary" teachings was not articulated until much later than Thomas. Komonchak states, with respect to *Humanae Vitae*:

> An important objection asks: If *Humanae Vitae* does not require assent, is there any teaching of the ordinary magisterium of the Pope which must be considered to require assent? It can be replied that *Humanae Vitae* does require assent, in the sense outlined above; that is, the fact that the encyclical comes from the supreme teacher in the Church, whose office was instituted by Christ and is guided by the Holy Spirit, establishes a presumption in favor of its truth. Therefore, assent to it can be suspended only because serious, personally convincing arguments lead a person to believe that the general presumption is not verified in this instance (1982:80).

Curran states the situation regarding noninfallible teaching in similar words:

> Noninfallible teaching calls for *obsequium religiosum* (religious submission or assent or respect) of intellect and will. However, unlike the assent of faith, this assent is not absolute or metaphysically certain. According to generally accepted theological interpretations, there is a presumption of truth in favor of such teaching

and the Catholic must make a sincere effort to give it intellectual assent; but such teaching can be erroneous (1987:28).

Our interest here is solely in noninfallible moral teaching. It calls for religious submission or assent but not absolute submission. Responsible decision-making, in the last analysis, is done based on individual conscience formed by spiritual direction, meditation, and study. But, as we have noted, American Catholicism has not been articulate on this question, causing confusion in many places.

Let us return to the survey results. We have seen that most American Catholics believe final moral authority on sex and marriage should be with the individual or with a collaboration of church leaders and individuals. Do personal characteristics such as age, sex, education, region of the country, and frequency of Mass attendance affect this attitude? We broke down the survey responses to see, and the results are in Table 4.2.

For the sake of simplicity the table shows the percentage who say that church leaders should be the final authority, and the four columns depict four of the moral issues. (The findings on the other two, not shown, are similar.) Looking first at age, we see major differences in attitudes between young and old; the division occurs between the 55-and-over group and those younger. Among the three young age groups there are no notable differences. Figure 4.1 graphs the age differences.

Catholics over 55 adhere much more to traditional church authority than those under 55, and this has implications for the future: in twenty years many in the over-55 group will be gone. In further analysis, not shown here, we made more detailed age breakdowns to see exactly where the greatest disjunction in attitudes occurs. We found smoother age-difference curves than Figure 4.1 suggests. In general, Catholics over 50 are measurably different than those under 50, and the most traditional are those over 60.

Table 4.2
Percentage Saying "Church Leaders" Should Have The Final Say
About Right Or Wrong

	Sexual Relations Outside Marriage	Homo-sexual Behavior	Divorce Remarrying Without Annulment	Practicing Contraceptive Birth Control
All:	34	32	23	12
Age: 18-29	22	29	17	10
30-39	29	24	16	7
40-54	30	27	17	12
55 or over	51	47	37	20
Education:				
Some High School	-- *	38	--	--
High School Graduate	--	34	--	--
Some College or Vocational School	--	29	--	--
College Graduate or More	--	26	--	--
Importance of the Catholic Church to you personally:				
The most important part of my life	54	50	41	35
Among the most important parts	42	35	25	11
Quite important, but so are other areas of my life	25	29	18	8
Not terribly important to me, or not very important to me	14	15	10	7
Frequency of Mass Attendance:				
At least weekly	45	45	30	20
Almost every week, or monthly	28	25	20	9
Seldom or never	19	18	13	4
Region:				
New England, Middle Atlantic	--	35	23	14
East North Central	--	26	20	12
West North Central	--	27	27	12
Southeast, South Central	--	21	15	2
Southwest	--	49	30	17
Mountain, Pacific	--	29	21	12

*Breakdowns with less than 12 percentage point differences are not shown.

This finding has some implications. Will the young Catholics turn more conservative as they grow older? In repeated studies, sociologists have found little evidence to support the widespread belief that people grow more conservative with age. The reason the notion is widely held, in spite of lack of empirical support, is that yesterday's liberal viewpoint on many issues is often today's conservative viewpoint. But the attitudes *of individuals* generally change little—it is the change in social context which gives this appearance (see Cutler and Kaufman, 1975; Glenn, 1980; Braungart and Braungart, 1986). Most of the research is on political attitudes, but the findings apply to moral issues as well. Given this prospect, we must expect a reduction in acceptance of church

Figure 4.1
Age Groups Saying Moral Authority To Decide What Is Right Or Wrong Rests With Church Leaders (Percents)

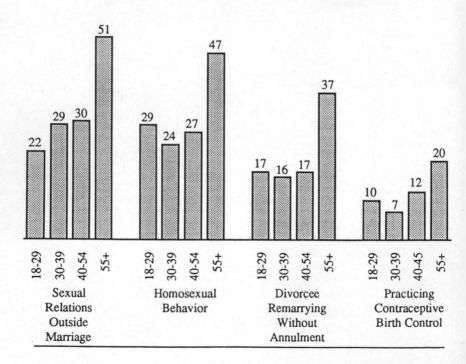

authority on sex and marriage questions in the next twenty years (assuming no change in the church teachings). This is one of the important findings of the 1987 survey.

Table 4.2 also shows differences by level of education. To our surprise they were not very large. This suggests that the shifts in Catholic attitudes are broad-based, not just limited to an educated subgroup. They cannot be attributed solely to the impact of higher education, but rather to broader influences in the total Catholic community. The shifts are especially noticeable among Catholics in their twenties, thirties, and forties.

Lower in the table are two series of figures showing whether levels of accepted authority vary according to the importance of the Church to the respondent and the respondent's frequency of Mass attendance. They both have the same pattern: there is a strong association between these indicators and attitudes toward church authority. Catholics to whom the Church is quite important and who attend Mass regularly accord much more authority to the Church on sex and marriage issues than do other Catholics. The question arises whether these patterns are merely a reflection of age differences. That is, it could be that older Catholics (a) find the Church more important and attend Mass more often, and also (b) accord more moral authority to the Church. If this is the case, possibly age explains everything, and the explanatory power of "importance of the Church" or Mass attendance is minimal. We checked this by controlling for age when looking at the relationship between Mass attendance and attitudes about Church authority. The relationships held up strongly, indicating that Mass attendance is a predictor of the attitudes even apart from age. Put simply, both older age and more frequent Mass attendance (or alternately, a greater importance of the Church) are predictors of willingness to accept Church authority.

The bottom of Table 4.2 shows variations by region. Originally we looked at eight different regions, but since some were similar in attitude we collapsed them into six. Note that the Southwest has the strongest support for church authority of any region, and the Southeast plus South

Central (south of the Mason-Dixon line and east of the Mississippi River) has the weakest. The explanation for this is unclear, and all we can do is speculate that the Old South had few Catholics until the last thirty years, when well-educated Catholics migrated south as managers in the new industry there. This has made the South, along with the West, a liberal sector in American Catholicism. Why the West came out *less* individualistic in attitudes is unclear. It has proven to be *more* individualistic than other regions in numerous surveys in recent years, but not here. In any event, no region had as high as 50 percent saying that church leaders should have the final say about right or wrong.

Possibly regional differences are reflections of nationality differences. We asked: "From what nationality group, or groups, are you mainly descended? (If more than one:) Which was the main one?" Not everyone could name one, but 89 percent did so, and we compared the largest nationality groups in their attitudes on church authority. We found the Polish to be the most supportive of church moral authority; no single group can be identified as the least supportive.

Not shown in Table 4.2 are three variables which we looked at, but which turned out to be unrelated to the attitudes. They are gender, amount of income, and amount of Catholic education at each of three levels—elementary, secondary, and higher education. None had a noteworthy effect.

Rights of Catholic Laity in Church Decisions

Another portion of the survey was devoted to a topic which has implications for church authority. It asked whether Catholic laity should or should not have the right to participate in church decisions. Here the overt issue is not who has final moral authority, but rather who should participate in framing church moral teachings (which will carry some authority). We can assume that church teachings formulated in a process having lay support will enjoy more accepted authority than those made in a process without support. But which process would be the most acceptable?

This section of the survey began: "For each of the following areas of church life, please tell me if you think the Catholic laity should have the right to participate, or should not have the right to participate." The interviewer asked about eleven areas, of which five are pertinent in this chapter. See Table 4.3. At the top are three sex-related moral issues. The respondents are split roughly half-and-half on whether or not laity should participate. The issue on which the respondents most favored lay participation is birth control—probably because just about all lay adults must confront this issue, and it has far-reaching consequences. Otherwise the respondents are divided about half-and-half, with one group saying the important moral decisions should be made by church leaders without laity and the other saying that laity have the right to participate.

Table 4.3

In These Areas Of Church Life, Should The Catholic Laity Have The Right To Participate, Or Not? (Percents)

	Laity Should	Laity Should Not	Not Sure
Deciding Moral Issues			
Making church policy about divorce	50	44	6
Making church policy about birth control	53	40	8
Making policies about homosexual behavior	39	50	11
Deciding Institutional Church Issues			
Deciding whether women should be ordained to the priesthood	48	46	6
Deciding whether priests should be allowed to marry	46	45	8

The bottom part of the table includes two issues facing the institutional Church, shown for comparison. Both are important worldwide ecclesiastical questions (though they relate as well to issues of sexuality and gender). Does it matter if the issue up for decision has to do with institutional questions rather than moral teachings? Apparently not, since the responses in the bottom of the table are similar to those in the top.

Are there clear patterns among Catholics as to who do or do not want laity to participate in these decisions? We computed breakdowns, as before. Table 4.4 depicts the percentages who said that the laity *should* have the right to participate.

The age pattern is the same as we saw in Table 4.2: the older Catholics tend to say that laity should not participate, while the younger ones say laity should. The main difference in views occurs between those older than 55 and those younger than 55, as we saw before.

Differences by level of education are larger than we saw earlier. On four out of the five items they are large enough to be noteworthy. The main shift occurs between those with less than a high-school diploma and those with a high-school diploma or more; the latter want more lay participation. (Having been to college or not makes little difference.) This pattern has been found repeatedly in sociological research—that people without a high-school diploma have relatively less experience of participation in community organizations and committees. As more and more Catholics complete high school in future years, we expect that the percentage believing laity should participate in these church decisions will rise.

The breakdowns by importance of the Church and by frequency of Mass attendance have patterns similar to those in Table 4.2, except that the impact of Mass attendance here is much weaker than the impact of the importance of the Church. Why is this? For whatever reason, the more important a Catholic layperson feels the Church is in his or her life, the *less* he or she wants laity to participate in church decision-making.

Table 4.4
Percentage Saying Catholic Laity Should Have The Right To
Participate In Each Area of Church Life

	Policy on Divorce	Policy on Birth Control	Policy Homo-sexual Behavior	Whether Women are Ordained	Whether Priests Should Marry
All:	50	53	39	48	46
Age: 18-29	60	62	47	56	55
30-39	52	58	46	54	51
40-54	53	56	35	49	48
55 or over	36	36	29	32	33
Education:					
Some High School	-- *	46	26	36	35
High School Graduate	--	49	45	49	49
Some College or Vocational School	--	58	40	53	50
College Graduate or More	--	61	41	54	49
Importance of the Catholic Church to your personally:					
The most important part of my life	28	35	27	33	31
Among the most important parts	49	51	37	43	41
Quite important, but so are other areas of my life	54	55	45	52	49
Not terribly important to me, or not very important to me	64	69	44	65	68
Frequency of Mass Attendance:					
At least weekly	42	43	--	--	41
Almost every week, or monthly	55	59	--	--	47
Seldom or never	59	62	--	--	55
Region:					
New England, Middle Atlantic	49	53	--	47	50
East North Central	58	54	--	51	52
West North Central	57	60	--	54	43
Southeast, South Central	46	60	--	42	35
Southwest	40	38	--	45	38
Mountain, Pacific	49	53	--	47	43

*Breakdowns with less that 12 percentage point differences are not shown.

It is a curious state of affairs. People who see the Church as less important to them favor more lay participation, possibly because they disagree with some aspects of the institutional Church today, or possibly because they accept less church authority and believe lay participation will make church teachings more relevant to life today. Laypersons with strongest feelings about the institutional Church oppose any change, possibly because they perceive change as a threat or possibly because they see lay religious commitment in terms of personal devotions, not organizational participation. This raises a crucial question which we cannot answer with available information: if the Church allowed greater lay participation in these decisions, would the overall level of church commitment go up or go down? One could speculate that it would go up, since then the laity who are now lukewarm would feel more included, hence more supportive. One could also speculate that it would go down, since the increased lay participation would alienate many persons for whom the Church is now one of the most important things in their lives and who cherish the traditional model. We have no way of knowing the overall effect.

As before, we controlled for age to see if the relationships with Mass attendance remained the same. They did, indicating that age and Mass attendance (as well as self-reported importance of the Church) are separate in their influence on attitudes about lay participation.

Variations by region are shown at the bottom of Table 4.4. The differences are small, but in general the region most opposed to lay participation is the Southwest. The breakdown by nationality (not shown) found that the groups most opposed to lay participation in decision-making are the Polish and Hispanics. The group most in favor is the Irish, but only slightly so. Gender, income level, and amount of Catholic education had little effect on the attitudes.

Conclusions

The 1987 survey agrees with all others done in the last twenty years in showing that acceptance of church authority on many sexual issues, especially birth control, is weak. A majority of Catholics believe that on questions related to sex, final moral authority should remain with the individual or with a combination of church leaders and laity working together. Observers have been predicting that a collapse of moral authority on one topic will be contagious, affecting other topics before long, since laypersons will conclude that the system is flawed, hence view all its statements with skepticism. We find the argument plausible, though we have not seen any empirical proof.

An important finding, in our estimation, was that many Catholics think the final say about what is moral or immoral behavior should be with "individuals and leaders working together." This turns the spotlight to *process;* the present-day problems of church moral authority should perhaps be seen in these terms. Careful attention to the process of formulating church teachings and of making specific moral decisions would probably improve the acceptance of church moral authority. This entails no theological change, since the importance of the *sensus fidelium* of the people of the universal Church for clarifying moral truth has been accepted for centuries.

Several people have conjectured that the respondents' endorsement of "individuals and leaders working together" was increased by the recent experience of American bishops, who in the last six years have crafted three major pastoral letters on moral questions through the use of widely-inclusive public hearings and debate. Our research provides no proof that American laity have been influenced by this experience, but we believe it is very possible. The public attention and acclaim given the pastoral letters on nuclear war and the American economy have been enormous—unprecedented in the history of American Catholicism. Surely this experience has affected the views of American laity about the best processes for decision-making.

Our data strongly suggest that there will be a continued loss of moral authority by the hierarchy on sexual issues in the years ahead. This is predictable, since young people differ from their elders, and as the elders die and young people age, there will be a gradual overall attitude shift away from acceptance of unilateral church authority and toward more reliance on individual conscience. In addition, as education levels rise there will be more pressures for lay participation in church decision-making.

Another important finding in this regard was that Catholics who deem the Church very important in their lives disproportionately accept traditional church moral authority in sexual matters. The survey does not tell why this is the case. Maybe the most traditionally devout Catholics have been brought up to accept formal church teachings without question and want things to remain that way. Maybe people disgruntled by past moral teachings have pulled back from church commitment and Mass attendance. Maybe people most imbued with the individualistic tendencies of modern America for other reasons keep their distance from both the institutional Church and also its claim to moral authority. All these reasons have been argued by observers, but we cannot discern their truth or falsity. Whatever the reason, there would be both a gain and a loss in church commitment if Catholic church leaders reformulated their teachings about moral authority so as to affirm individual conscience more strongly or to include laity in church decision-making. This would improve their moral influence for some laity (especially the younger) but weaken it for others (many of the older).

This study, like all scientific work, provides no help on basic value questions, such as whether church moral authority in general is a good or bad thing. Our comments on this question come from experience and reflection, not from research. But it seems worthwhile to say that we believe church moral authority in the modern world is a good, even a precious, thing. In a world split into east and west blocs and into rich nations and poor nations—each with their own propaganda machines and attempts at thought control—an independent moral voice speaking God's will for humanity, as best it can be discerned, would be redemptive for all. So the proper agenda before the Church, in our view, is how to fulfill this promise. The job is, as we noted earlier, not just making statements about church teachings, but doing it in a way which increases the accepted authority of the statements. The people need to feel confident that the statements are validly grounded in the Gospel and that they speak for all of the People of God, free of special interests or parochial agendas. The worldwide Catholic Church is admirably situated for having an impact at this level, since it is independent of any national suzerainty and represents Catholics living in the socialistic East, the capitalistic West, the rich North, and the poor South. To illustrate this advantage, compare the situation of the Protestant churches, which are largely identified with this or that nation and whose worldwide structures, such as the World Council of Churches, are fragile. Their ability to make credible moral statements for all humanity, and to cause the statements to be taken seriously by the faithful, is much weaker.

The task is a momentous one, and our research and other experiences provide only two suggestions for helping with it. The first is the emphasis, noted above, on adjusting the *processes* of formulating Catholic moral teachings to include as much broad participation and open debate as possible. As proven in the case of the American bishops, this has the promise of achieving a more convincing result with broader acceptance in the total Catholic population. The second is a renewed analysis and discussion of the relationship between official church teachings and the well-informed private conscience in arriving at moral decisions, both at the general level of policy and at the personal level of private decisions. American Catholics would appreciate the clarification. A renewed appreciation of Church moral authority on crucial life-questions could benefit the People of God.

References

Bellah, Robert N., et al. 1985. *Habits of the Heart: Individualism and Commitment in American Life*. New York: Harper and Row.

Braungart, Richard G., and Margaret M. Braungart. 1986. "Life-Course and Generational Politics." *Annual Review of Sociology* 12:205-31.

Canon Law Society of America. 1983. *The Code of Canon Law: Latin-English Edition.* Washington, DC: Canon Law Society.

Curran, Charles E. 1985. *Directions in Fundamental Moral Theology.* Notre Dame, IN: University of Notre Dame Press.

_____. 1987. "Authority and Dissent in the Catholic Church." Pp. 27-34 in *Vatican Authority and American Catholic Dissent*, edited by William W. May. New York: Crossroad.

Cutler, Steven J., and Robert L. Kaufman. 1975. "Cohort Changes in Political Attitudes: Tolerance of Ideological Nonconformity." *Public Opinion Quarterly* 39:69-81.

Gallup, George, Jr., and Jim Castelli. 1987. *The American Catholic People: Their Beliefs, Practices, and Values.*Garden City, NY: Doubleday.

Glenn, Norval D. 1980. "Values, Attitudes, and Beliefs." Pp. 596-640 in *Constancy and Change in Human Development*, edited by Orville G. Brim and Jerome Kagan. Cambridge: Harvard University Press.

Greeley, Andrew M., William C. McCready, and Kathleen McCourt. 1976. *Catholic Schools in a Declining Church.* Kansas City: Sheed and Ward.

Hennesey, James. 1981. *American Catholics: A History of the Roman Catholic Community in the United States.* New York: Oxford University Press.

Komonchak, Joseph A. 1982. "Ordinary Papal Magisterium and Religious Assent." Pp. 67-90 in *Readings in Moral Theology, No. 3*, edited by Charles Curran and Richard McCormick. New York: Paulist Press.

_____. 1987. "Authority and Magisterium." Pp. 103-114 in *Vatican Authority and American Catholic Dissent*, edited by William W. May. New York: Crossroad.

Lasswell, Harold D., and Abraham Kaplan. 1950. *Power and Society: A Framework for Political Inquiry.* New Haven: Yale University Press.

Los Angeles Times. 1987. "Research Report on August 14-19 Nationwide Poll #128." Xeroxed research report.

Neuhaus, Richard John. 1987. *The Catholic Moment.* New York: Harper and Row.

New York Times. 1986. "Church Calls Excommunicated Catholic Abortion 'Accomplice'. " January 25.

Nisbet, Robert A. 1966. *The Sociological Tradition.* New York: Basic Books.

Providence Journal. 1986. "Priest Attempts to Clarify Rules on Who May Be Excommunicated." January 23, p. A6.

Rieff, Philip. 1966. *The Triumph of the Therapeutic: Uses of Faith After Freud.* New York: Harper.

Weakland, Rembert. 1986. "The Church in Worldly Affairs: Tensions Between Laity and Clergy." *America* 155:10 (October), 201.

Weber, Max. 1947. *The Theory of Social and Economic Organization.* Glencoe: Free Press.

5.

Democratization: A Dilemma for American Catholics?

Picture the following scene:

Soon after the death of their bishop, representatives of the Roman Catholic clergy and laity of the diocese gather together to elect the bishop's successor. The clergy and laity assembled for the election come from duly constituted representative bodies, such as pastoral councils, the priests' senate, and similar groups. After a lengthy discussion, each cleric and layperson casts his or her vote, and the person with the highest number of votes is declared the new bishop of the diocese. Preparations for the candidate's consecration to the episcopate are begun immediately, so that he can take office as soon as possible. At the same time, the results of the election are relayed to the Pope in Rome, who wastes no time in welcoming the new bishop as the leader of the diocese and as a new member of the college of bishops.

The reader might think that the scenario above is taken from a chapter in a novel or from a scene in a futuristic movie. After all, *everyone knows* that in the Roman Catholic Church it is a "divine right" for the Pope to appoint bishops. Who ever heard of clergy, and even more so, of laity having a say in electing their bishop? We look to the historical record for an answer to this supposedly rhetorical question.

The Selection of Bishops: An Historical View

Believe it or not, elections similar to the one depicted above did indeed take place all over the world during the first thousand years of the Church's existence. As Küng (*New York Times,* January 28, 1971) reminds us: "Some of the most outstanding bishops in all church history, men like Ambrose and Augustine, were decisively selected by the people."

Another reminder of this practice of the early Church comes from St. Cyprian (210-258), who was chosen bishop "by the judgment of God and the favor of the people." Cyprian offers the following testimony about elections in the early Church (cited in O'Meara, 1971:26):

It comes from divine authority that a bishop be chosen in the presence of the people before the eyes of all and that he be approved as worthy and fit by public judgment and testimony. . . . The Lord orders the bishop to be appointed before the whole synagogue, that is, He instructs and shows that priestly ordinations ought not to be performed except with the knowledge of the people present that, in the presence of the people, either the crimes of the evildoers may be revealed or the merits of the good may be proclaimed and that the ordination which has been examined by the suffrage and judgment of all may be just and lawful.

A further testimony regarding the right of the people to participate in the selection of a bishop can be found in the words of Leo the Great, who was pope from 440-461. Leo wrote: "He who is to preside over all must be elected by all." As O'Meara (1971:28) puts it, "Popular selection (of bishops) remained deeply rooted in the self-consciousness of the

Christians in the West." In fact, only towards the end of the first millenium did the Pope begin to enter the selection process outside Italy.

Looking closer to home, remember that it was only 200 years ago that John Carroll, the first bishop of the United States, was elected to that position by his own clergy. On March 12, 1788, a committee appointed by the clergy of the United States sent a petition to Pius VI, asking not only that an episcopal see be erected in this country, but also that, at least for the first time, the clergy be given the privilege of electing their own bishop. Soon after the Pope approved such an election, the priests met at Whitemarsh, Maryland, in May 1789, and elected John Carroll as the first bishop of the new see which they chose to be located at Baltimore. Pius VI ratified the election of John Carroll. In fact, "he was even pleased that the clergy had concurred with the choice he had made when he had appointed Carroll superior of the missions (in the United States) in 1784" (Trisco, 1971:43).

Two years later, however, when Bishop Carroll requested in his own name as well as that of his priests the same privilege for the election of the second bishop as coadjutor of Baltimore, the Vatican refused the request. Nonetheless, according to Trisco (1971:44), because "a direct appointment by Rome might be interpreted by the enemies of the Church in the young republic as a violation of the spirit of the Constitution," Carroll was informed that he should "consult with the older and more prudent priests of the diocese and propose any priest in the American mission whom you think fit and capable; the Holy Father will then appoint him coadjutor with all necessary and reasonable faculties."

At the time of the birth of our nation, then, Church authorities in Rome were cognizant of the American value of democratic procedures and made some concessions. But these concessions were subsequently withdrawn, and since 1893 the Pope's apostolic delegate in Washington, D.C. has overseen the process of the selection of bishops. Let us look at the practice today.

The Selection of Bishops: Current Norms and Practices

Canon 377 of the Code of Canon Law (1983:139) states: "The Supreme Pontiff freely appoints bishops or confirms those who have been legitimately elected." The canon further stipulates that every three years the bishops are to compose a list of priests suitable for the episcopacy and send it to the Apostolic See. In the event that a bishop is to be named, it is the responsibility of the pontifical legate to seek out suggestions of the metropolitan of the diocese, the president of the conference of bishops, and to "communicate them to the Apostolic See together with his own preference."

The election of the bishop, therefore, has clearly been taken out of the hands of the laity and even of those clergy below the rank of bishop. There is, however one clause in Canon 377 which mentions a possible participation of clergy and laity. It reads thus: "Moreover, the pontifical legate is to hear some members of the college of consultors and of the cathedral chapter, and *if he judges it expedient* (emphasis ours), he shall also obtain, individually and in secret, the opinion of other members of the secular and religious clergy as well as the laity who are outstanding for their wisdom."

Finally, Canon 378 places the ultimate responsibility for the selection of bishops squarely in the Pope's hands when it states: "The definitive judgment concerning the suitability of the person to be promoted belongs to the Apostolic See."

While some American Catholics are in agreement that the Pope should select their bishops, others have taken a different position. One of those who recently voiced his concern regarding the nonparticipation of the local Church in the selection of bishops is Rev. M. Edmund Hussey, pastor of Saint Paul Church, Yellow Springs, Ohio, who, in a talk given to a group of priests, said (Hussey,1988:16):

I do not hold a brief for a particular method of choosing bishops and definitely not for a popular election of bishops. But I do believe that the local Church should have an open, clear, and effective role in the selection of its bishop. I also strongly believe that American bishops should be chosen by the American Church in a well-defined manner and then confirmed by Rome, instead of chosen by Rome in a mysterious manner and only then accepted by an American diocese.

Why did the way of selecting bishops change over the centuries, progressively excluding laity and priests? O'Meara (1971:31-32), citing cultural rather than dogmatic reasons, argues:

With the entrance into the Church of large masses of people and the turmoil of the barbarian invasions the idea of the Christian community as a Spirit-directed, realistic community of mature religious men and women was compromised. Ideas such as freedom, collegiality and pluralism-with-unity found no atmosphere in which to be nourished. The bishop, and the man to be bishop, were necessarily viewed in a minimalist way. The creative and pastoral leader of a dynamic community had to be sacrificed for a basic, static focal point of church life amidst the primitive ambition and upheaval of the times.

Social and cultural conditions have changed many times over since the turmoil of the barbarian invasions, and the Church has always been slow to respond to change. However, Pope John XXIII utilized his papal authority to promote changes in the Church in two ways: by summoning the bishops of the world to participate in the second Vatican Council, and by ordering a revision of the Code of Canon Law.

The ideal of collegiality was not only revived during the deliberations of the Second Vatican Council, but, more importantly, it also became the major theme of the Council through Pope John XXIII's stress on the need for co-responsibility. In the years since the last session of Vatican II in 1965, the impact of the stress on collegiality has been felt by clergy and laity alike in Catholic dioceses throughout the world. In the next section, we focus on its impact at the level closest to home—the local parish.

Collegiality at the Parish Level: Current Norms and Practices

In its first and deepest meaning, collegiality means community (Mc-Brien, 1971:17-18). Therefore within the local churches, it refers to a close bond among bishops, priests, and the laity as a whole. Vatican II, however, focused on the second meaning of collegiality, which refers to the relationship between the pope and other bishops. According to this meaning the pope, when he acts as head of the Church, always acts as head and member of the college of bishops, and never as a purely private person. Therefore, without prejudice to the rights and prerogatives of the pope, "all bishops in hierarchical communion share in the responsibility for the universal Church" (*Christus Dominus*, n.5) and are thereby "the subjects of supreme and full power over the universal Church" (*Lumen Gentium*, n. 22 and n. 27).

How is collegiality translated to the relationship between priest and laity in the local parish? In what ways do parishioners share in the responsibility for the parish? And what are some of the changes in norms and practices which have made this collegiality possible at the local parish level? In keeping with the Vatican II changes, the revised Code of Canon Law allows for the expansion of lay participation, and thus for a sharing of responsibility. Canon 129 (1983:41) states:

> In accord with the prescriptions of the law, those who have received sacred orders are capable of the power of governance, which exists in the Church by divine institition and is also called the power of jurisdiction. *Lay members of the Christian faithful can cooperate in the exercise of this power in accord with the norm of law.* (Emphasis ours.)

Thus the power of governance or jurisdiction can be shared by the laity. What the law allows is a cooperation between priest and laity in the exercise of this power. Because this can be interpreted as a sharing of responsibility, we can label this as collegiality on the parish level.

An additional statement in Canon 228, which also allows for greater lay participation in assuming certain ecclesiastical offices and functions, was quoted in Chapter 1 (see p. 19). There are some activities, however, which are explicitly prohibited by Canon Law. For instance, the new Code makes it very clear that laity are not acceptable as homilists, for it states that the eucharistic homily is exclusively the prerogative of ordained priests and deacons. A strict interpretation of the law would, however, allow for a layperson to give a sermon at the end of Mass, after the reception of holy communion (*National Catholic Reporter*, December 25, 1987:21).

Within certain limitations, then, there are some new roles being offered to the laity. For example, instead of the priests performing all of the parish activities, some laity have taken on specialized roles such as directors of religious education, extraordinary ministers of the Eucharist, lectors, and parish associates in charge of youth ministry and liturgical planning. Many laity have also participated as members of parish councils.

How, if at all, do these changes at the parish level, which were made possible by Vatican II and the new Code of Canon Law, relate to the laity's thinking about the need for more democratization in the Church? Let's consult our 1987 survey data to see.

Democratic Decision-Making: Vatican, Diocesan, and Parish Levels

In our national survey of lay Catholics, we asked: "Some people think the Catholic Church should have more democratic decision-making in church affairs that do not involve matters of faith than it has at present. Do you favor or oppose this idea (a) at the local parish level, (b) at the diocesan level, and (c) at the level of the Vatican ?"

Our wording of this question purposely ruled out the issue of more democratic decision-making in church affairs involving matters of faith, such as the nature of the resurrection or the meaning of the Eucharist. We qualified the question in this way because it was meant to be a general question about whether the respondents favored or opposed greater participation of the laity in church affairs involving moral and/or institutional issues, such as making church policy about birth control or deciding whether women should be ordained to the priesthood. At each level, we asked if they favored, opposed, or were unsure about more democratic decision-making in the Church.

The results are shown in Table 5.1. A majority of the laity think that the Catholic Church should have more democratic decision-making at the local parish level, at the diocesan level, and at the level of the Vatican. They are slightly more likely to favor more democratic decision-making at the parish level. Only at the level of the Vatican do as many as 30% of the laity oppose the idea.

Table 5.1
Should The Church Have More Democratic Decision-Making?
(Percents)

	Favor	Oppose	Unsure
At the local parish level	60	27	13
At the diocesan level	55	28	17
At the Vatican level	51	30	19

Table 5.2 shows how the factors of age, education, and income affect the general responses of the laity. With regard to age, we see the sharpest differences in attitudes between young and old; most of the division occurs between the 55-and-over age group and those under 55. The three younger age groups are very similar with respect to favoring more democratic decision-making at the local parish and diocesan levels. But those in the 40-54 age group resemble their elders more when it comes to attitudes regarding democratic decision-making at the level of the Vatican. At all three levels, the largest differences are between those in their 30s and the oldest age group. The main message is that a majority of those under 55 years of age favor the idea that the Church should have more democratic decision-making at the local parish, diocesan, and

Table 5.2
Percentage Favoring The Idea That The Church Should Have More Democratic Decision-Making

		Parish	Diocese	Vatican
All:		60	55	51
Age:	18-29	64	58	54
	30-39	66	62	59
	40-54	64	58	49
	55 or over	46	44	44
Education:				
	Some High School	38	30	34
	High School Graduate	58	55	53
	Some College or Vocational School	72	69	58
	College Graduate or More	74	69	60
Income:				
	Under $10,000	39	34	31
	$10,000-$19,999	62	52	55
	$20,000-$29,999	67	62	52
	$30,000-39,999	58	59	62
	$40,000 and over	69	68	59

Vatican levels, while slightly less than a majority in the 55 and over age group favor the idea. A closer examination of this older age group showed that about one-third oppose the idea, and one-fifth are unsure.

Education also makes a difference, as our data show. The more highly educated favor more democratic decision-making. The two highest levels (some college and college graduates) are very similar, and there is a striking difference between them and the group with less than high, school education. Even the middle group (high-school graduates), however, has a majority in favor. Table 5.2 also shows differences by level of income. The major difference here is between those whose annual household income before taxes is under $10,000 and the rest of the sample, that is, those whose income is $10,000 or over. The lowest income group is much less likely to favor more democratic decision-making at all three levels; only about one-third are in favor compared to over half of the respondents in all of the higher income groups. However, this finding should not be interpreted to mean that two-thirds of the lower income group *oppose* the idea. Rather, our data show that the lower income group is almost evenly split on this question; about 30% oppose the idea and about 30% are unsure at all three levels.

In sum: the majority of the laity are consistently in favor of increased democratic decision-making in their local parishes, in their dioceses, and in Rome. Younger age groups, those with at least a high-school education, and higher income groups have the highest percentages favoring the idea. (See Figure 5.1 on decision-making in parishes.)

Not shown in Table 5.2 is a comparison by gender, which showed that men and women were very similar on this item. We also computed comparisons by importance of the Church to them and by frequency of Mass attendance, but there were no significant differences on these comparisons, either. This means that Catholic laity favor more democratic participation in Church life regardless of their level of commitment or frequency of Mass attendance. On this matter, there is no "silent majority" in opposition.

Figure 5.1
Percent Favoring More Democratic Decision-Making in Parishes

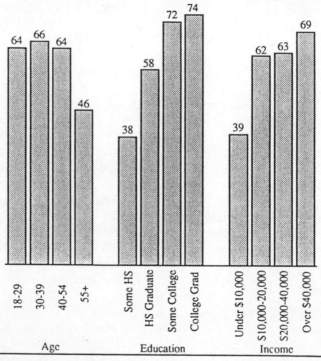

Given Pope John Paul's deep concerns about the American Church, and the intervention of the Holy Office in several notable cases (e.g., Hunthausen, Curran, and the signers of the pro-choice ad), we decided to ask what the laity thought the relationship should be between the Vatican and the American bishops. The question was worded thus: "Here is a question about the American Catholic bishops. Should the American bishops become more independent or less independent from the Vatican and the Pope in the way they run the Catholic Church in America, or should the situation remain as it is now?" The response categories were: more, less, same, or don't know.

The results are presented in Table 5.3. Overall only one in three said the bishops should become more independent, while 49% said the situation should remain the same, 10% said "less," and 9% replied that they did not know. Table 5.3 also shows the impact of such social characteristics as age, education, income, and importance of the Church.

Table 5.3

Percentage Saying The American Bishops Should Be More Independent From The Vatican In The Way They Run The Church In America

		Bishops More Independent
All:		32
Age:	18-29	31
	30-39	43
	40-54	34
	55 or more	23
Education:		
	Some High School	23
	High School Graduate	31
	Some College or Vocational School	39
	College Graduate or More	38
Income:		
	Under $10,000	26
	$10,000-$19,999	33
	$20,000-$29,999	31
	$30,000-$39,999	35
	$40,000 and over	40
How important is the Catholic Church to you personally?		
	The most important part of my life	20
	Among the most important parts	31
	Quite important to me, but so are other areas of my life	35
	Not terribly important, or not very important to me at all	40

Looking first at the age groups, we see that the laity in their 30s are more likely than any of the other age groups to say that the bishops should be more independent. As expected, those aged 55 and over were the least likely to support more independence.

Regarding educational attainment, the notable difference again is between those with the least amount of education (some high school) and those with at least some college. A similar pattern is found among the income groups, where the middle-level groups are very similar. The only difference worth mentioning among the income groups is that between the lowest and the highest income levels, 26% and 40% respectively. Laity with annual household incomes of $40,000 and over are significantly more likely than those in the lowest income group to say that the American bishops should be more independent from the Vatican.

Finally, looking at the breakdowns on importance of the Church, we can see that there is a notable difference between the groups at either extreme. Those who said the Church is not terribly important or not important at all were much more likely to say the bishops should be more independent than those who said the Church is the most important part of their lives. We also examined the data on frequency of Mass attendance and on gender, but we found no relationship. Table 5.3's main message is that, with the exception of age, the significant differences are between the two extremes: some high school vs. college education, under $10,000 annual income vs. $40,000 and over, and those who view the Church as most important vs. those who view the Church as not terribly important to them at all. We should keep in mind, however, that only among those in their 30s do as many as 40% think the American Church should be more independent. Only a third of the laity said the American bishops should become more independent from Rome.

For the most part, the laity seem satisfied with the status quo. The range wanting more independence is from 20% to 43%, while they tend to cluster around 30%. The largest group wants no change from the present.

Democratization Issues: Parish Finances and Selection of Priests

Another portion of the 1987 survey was devoted to a topic directly re-lated to the democratization issue: the right of the laity to participate in various areas of church life. In order to understand the thinking of the laity on this topic, we asked the following question: "For each of the fol-lowing areas of church life, please tell me if you think the Catholic laity should have the right to participate, or should not have the right to par-ticipate." The response categories were: should, should not, and not sure. In all, we included eleven areas of church life, some of which are discussed in other chapters in this book (see Chapter 4). Here we will discuss two of the areas pertinent to democratization: 1) deciding how parish income should be spent, and 2) selecting priests for their parish. Table 5.4 depicts the overall response on these two items.

Table 5.4

Should The Catholic Laity Have The Right To Participate?

(Percents)

	Should	Should Not	Unsure
Deciding how parish income should be spent	81	14	6
Selecting the priests for their parish	57	35	8

As we can see in Table 5.4, an overwhelming majority (81%) of our respondents said that the laity should have the right to participate in deciding how parish income should be spent. In addition, over half of the laity said that they should have the right to participate in selecting the priests for their parish, while a third said that the laity should not have this right.

There is no doubt that most lay Catholics think there should be more lay participation in decision-making regarding the spending of parish income and the selection of their parish priests. Table 5.5 shows how such social characteristics as age, education, income, importance of the Church in their lives, and frequency of Mass attendance help refine the basic findings.

The laity's plea for the right to participate holds across all age groups; the only notable difference with respect to spending of parish income is that between the oldest age group (74%) and the 30s cohort (86%). On the question of the right of the laity to participate in selecting their priests, we find somewhat the same pattern; the only important difference is that between the oldest (49%) and the youngest cohort (67%). Since we expect more traditional responses from older people, it is surprising that nearly half of them believe they should be allowed to participate in the selection of priests. With 42% of the laity 55 and over saying the laity should *not* have the right to participate, the oldest age cohort was found to be almost evenly divided on this issue.

Looking next at education, those with a college education (90%), most strongly support lay participation in decisions about the spending of parish income, but even those who did not complete high school were strongly supportive (73%). On the other hand, education did not make a difference on the issue of selecting parish priests.

With respect to spending parish income the familiar pattern emerges again at different income levels; the notable difference is between the lowest income group (72%) and the highest income group (89%). The pattern is much less clear on the question of selection of parish priests, however. Here the second highest income group, $30,000-$39,999, is different from all other income groups. They are the only one with less than a majority (44%) saying that the laity should have the right to participate, compared to about 60% of the other income groups. This finding seems anomalous.

Table 5.5

Percentage Saying Catholic Laity Should Have The Right To Participate In Each Area Of Church Life

		How Parish Income Is Spent	Selecting Parish Priests
All:		81	57
Age:	18-29	80	67
	30-39	86	59
	40-54	85	53
	55 or over	74	48
Education:			
	Some High School	73	--*
	High School Graduate	78	--
	Some College or Vocational School	87	--
	College Graduate or more	90	--
Income:			
	Under $10,000	72	57
	$10,000-$19,999	77	57
	$20,000-$29,999	83	62
	$30,000-$39,999	82	44
	$40,000 and over	89	59
How Important is the Catholic Church to you personally?			
	The most important part of my life	80	37
	Among the most important parts	83	57
	Quite important, but so are other areas of my life	82	62
	Not terribly important, or not very important to me at all	71	62
Frequency of Mass Attendance:			
	Weekly or oftener	--*	51
	Almost every week, or monthly	--	61
	Seldom or never	--	65

*Breakdowns with less than 12 percentage point differences are not shown.

Does church importance make a difference? Large majorities in all categories support the right of laity to participate in making decisions about spending parish income, with the range between 83% and 71%. The three groups who say the Church is important to them are very similar on the issue of the right of the laity to participate in decisions about spending parish income.

The pattern is different on the issue of the selection of parish priests. Here there is a striking difference between those who say the Church is the most important part of their lives and the other three groupings. Only 37% of the former say the Catholic laity should have the right to participate in selecting their parish priests, compared to 60% of the others. In fact, 54% of those saying the Church is most important to them think that the laity should *not* participate in the selection of parish priests. This finding is important as it is the only instance where a majority opposed the idea.

Finally, let's look at frequency of Mass attendance. There were no significant differences on the issue of spending parish income, but there was a significant difference between the most frequent Mass attenders and the least frequent attenders on the issue of priest selection. 51% of those attending Mass at least weekly said the laity should have the right to participate, compared to 65% of those who attend Mass seldom or never.

Not shown in Table 5.5 is a breakdown by gender, which turned out not to be a predictor variable. Men and women are very similar in their strong support of lay participation.

What is the primary message found in Table 5.5? There is a very strong plea from the laity regarding their right to participate in decisions about the spending of parish income, and this request is expressed with a louder voice from the younger, more educated, higher income groups, and also from those who say the Catholic Church is important to them. The secondary message with regard to the selection of parish priests could be described as a "mixed bag." While the plea for more participation from the younger groups and from infrequent Mass attenders is strong, on the other hand, those with incomes in the $30,000 range and those who say the Church is the most important part of their lives are less likely to favor the laity's right to participate in the selection of parish priests. It makes sense that people who go to Mass at least weekly would be more satisfied with the status quo, but even this group shows a majority (51%) in support of lay participation.

Discussion and Conclusion

We began this chapter by noting that both priests and laity participated in the selection of bishops in the early Church, and that priests did earlier in American history. The culmination of highly centralized authoritarianism came with the First Vatican Council in the nineteenth century, with its declaration of papal infallibility. However, in his convening of Vatican II and calling for a reform of the Code of Canon Law, Pope John XXIII attempted to turn the tide and open the Church to more collegiality. In our survey we wanted to find out the views of Catholic laity who are accustomed to democratic procedures in their political life, and to personal freedom in secular activities.

We found that lay Catholics want far more say in decision-making at all levels, especially in their parishes; they are also supportive, but to a lesser degree, of greater democratization at the diocesan and Vatican levels. The desire of the laity for more democratization at the local level than higher makes sense. They have had more experience seeing laity active locally. They may feel more hesitant about recommending lay involvement at the higher levels of church organization (the diocesan level and the Vatican), with which they have had less personal experience.

With regard to democratic decision-making at the parish level, we found that there could be some very important untapped lay resources at the Church's disposal, if those in power would permit lay men and women to make their contributions. If the laity could participate in decision-making at this level, parishes might find that they would have more assistance in a number of areas, including financial advice and the recruitment and selection of priests for parishes.

Can we predict that lay Catholics will continue to push for more democratic decision-making in the Church? As we noted in Chapter 1, Fichter (1977:163-164) made the observation ten years ago that the changes occurring in the Church are at the grass roots level, and that "dependence on legislation from above has largely switched to dependence on the conscience of the people."

Our data bear out Fichter's insights. Specifically, younger Catholics, both those under thirty and in their thirties, and those with college education, are most supportive of increased lay involvement in decision-making in the Church. If the trend of increased college attendance by Catholics continues, we can expect that the laity's push for greater say in church matters will intensify, even at the level of the diocese and the Vatican. The subtitle of this chapter asks a question. Is the democratization of the Catholic Church a dilemma for American Catholics? Our national survey of lay Catholics has suggested that it is. Living in a nation characterized by democratic values, and recognizing that the Church at the higher levels is operating as a monarchy, the majority of our lay Catholics are expressing that dilemma when they tell us that they want the laity to have greater participation in church decision-making at all levels. Inspired by Pope John XXIII, what the laity are asking for is a wider opening of the "windows" of the Catholic Church.

References

Fichter, Joseph H. 1977. "Restructuring Catholicism: Symposium on Thomas O'Dea." *Sociological Analysis* 38:163-64.

Hoge, Dean R. 1987. *The Future of Catholic Leadership: Responses to The Priest Shortage.* Kansas City, MO: Sheed & Ward.

Hussey, M. Edmund. 1988. "The Priesthood after the Council: Theological Reflections." *Church* 4:12-17.

John Paul II. 1983. *Code of Canon Law.* Washington, DC: Canon Law Society.

Küng, Hans. 1971. "Who Shall Choose the Bishops?" *New York Times* (January 28).

O'Meara, Thomas F. 1971. "Emergence and Decline of Popular Voice in the Selection of Bishops." Pp. 21-32 in *The Choosing of Bishops,* edited by William W. Bassett. Hartford, CT: Canon Law Society.

McBrien, Richard P. 1971. "A Preliminary Ecclesiological Statement." Pp. 11-20 in *The Choosing of Bishops,* edited by William W. Bassett. Hartford, CT: Canon Law Society.

Trisco, Robert F. 1971. "The Variety of Procedures in Modern History." Pp. 33-60 in *The Choosing of Bishops,* edited by William W. Bassett. Hartford, CT: Canon Law Society.

6.

Women in the Church: Limited Empowerment

Picture the following scene.

The time: pre-Vatican II. The place: a third-grade classroom in a Catholic school in the United States. Sister Mary has just announced that Latin lessons for new altar servers will begin this week and she asks how many students are interested. A few boys raise their hands, and beaming with pride, Sister Mary congratulates them and promises to help them with their Latin. Meanwhile, some of the girls who would aspire to be altar servers must sit on their hands, knowing that they cannot volunteer because, through no fault of their own, they belong to the wrong gender category.

In this scene what might a third-grade girl be thinking? What she understands is that some of her classmates will have the privilege of serving Mass, of assisting the priest inside the gates of the sanctuary. Although she has shared many other activities with the boys being chosen, and she believes that she could learn the Latin responses as well or better than most of them, this moment makes it crystal-clear to her that she cannot volunteer. She knows that during Mass only the priests and the altar boys are allowed in that sacred place. What this third grader might be wondering is whether she is inferior, profane, or somehow unclean because she happens to be a girl.

That same third-grade girl has probably observed that women are quite visible in her parish. They perform the traditional "female" tasks like teaching in the school, cleaning and ironing altar linens, baking cakes for church bazaars, cooking for church dinners, singing in the choir, and keeping house for the priests. Where women are not visible is in the performance of the more important "male" tasks like saying Mass, giving sermons, and administering church funds. In short, she can see that women have always been active within the parish through countless services, but they have been excluded from the most important activities. This does not seem inappropriate to her, however, for she can also see that women's activities in the Church mirror those in the home. Just as her father is head of the house, so the priest seems to be the head of the local church. Thus her expectations about gender roles have been formed at home and reinforced at church.

Now let's focus on another scene, which actually occurred about ten years ago, in October of 1979. This historic encounter took place at the Shrine of the Immaculate Conception, on the campus of Catholic University. It was there that Sister Theresa Kane expressed her concerns about the role of women in the Church to Pope John Paul II. It was not only Theresa Kane's position regarding women's participation in the Church which became the issue of contention, however; it was her apparent audacity. Some Catholics asked, "Who does she think she is, talking like that to the Holy Father?" Others applauded her intervention.

Theresa Kane challenged the taken-for-granted assumptions about women's "proper place" in the Church. That challenge was reiterated by laity, priests, and even some members of the hierarchy during the Pope's second visit to the United States in September, 1987. An example is found in the following words to Pope John Paul II spoken by Archbishop Rembert Weakland (1987:262):

. . . There are no words to explain so much pain on the part of so many competent women today who feel that they are second-class citizens in a Church they love. That pain turns easily to anger and is often shared and transmitted to the younger generation of men and women. Women do not want to be treated as stereotypes of sexual inferiority, but want to be seen as necessary to the full life of a Church that teaches and shows by example the co-discipleship of the sexes as instruments of God's kingdom. They seek a Church where the gifts of women are equally accepted and appreciated. Many of them do not yet see the Church imaging such a co-discipleship but fear that it is still one of male superiority and dominance.

These dramatic changes in thinking about the role of women in the Church are a pale reflection of the changes in women's roles and statuses in the larger society. Witness, for instance, the American woman's greater participation in the labor force, her higher educational attainment, and her involvement in the change movements of the 1960s and 1970s, especially in the women's movement. These external factors were important resources for the changes in Catholic woman's position in the Church, but equally important were internal changes, in particular Vatican II.

Our 1987 survey probed the laity's attitudes about expanding the participation of women in a number of ways. This chapter examines the changing role of women in the Catholic Church.

Vatican II and the Role of Women

Why does this chapter begin with the scene in the third-grade classroom? That scene sets the stage for the issues we will now discuss in this chapter. Many women who were in elementary school before Vatican II ended in 1965 had similar experiences which raised questions in their minds about where they fit in, and as they grew older some of them began to question whether their "appropriate place" in the Church would always be a subservient one. On the other hand, many women never questioned their position; their basic stance was that of an unquestioning obedience to church authority.

Have women always been placed in subordinate positions in the Church? A glance backward in time will help to answer this question. At one time in the early Christian Church abbesses wielded a considerable amount of power. Such power persisted in many cases until the 1800s. Morris (1973, cited in Wallace, 1975:295-296) documents the quasi-episcopal status of the abbess which included some or all of the following rights and duties: licensing bishops to exercise pontifical rites in her diocese; licensing priests to say Mass in her churches; absolving in cases of excommunications; establishing new parishes and rebuilding dilapidated churches; holding places in councils with a rank above the clergy; reading the gospel; suspending clergy subject to her; conferring of offices and benefices; promulgating dispensations and graces from Rome for her district or diocese; and even at one time, hearing confessions and preaching in public. Although women were never empowered to consecrate the Eucharist, the rights and duties of the abbess which we have just mentioned will probably seem astounding to the average Catholic today.

In the era preceding the reign of Pope John XXIII, there were some women in important positions, like administrators of Catholic hospitals, presidents of Catholic women's colleges, and principals of Catholic high schools and grammar schools. These were not roles reserved solely for the clergy, and the vast majority of women in these positions were members of religious communities. It is important to remember that Catholic Sisters, because they cannot receive the sacrament of Holy Orders, have never been members of the clergy. In a certain sense they are in a state of "limbo," neither clergy nor laity; but in the last analysis they are more similar to the laity, especially in terms of power in the Church.

The deliberations of Vatican II, which were influenced by Pope John XXIII's stress on co-responsibility, resulted in some attempts to bridge the chasm between clergy and laity, and even to address the issue of women's contributions. This is all the more surprising when one realizes that women were almost invisible at the Council among the 2500 male bishops, hundreds of priests invited as experts ("periti"), ecumenical representatives from other religions, and a few laity. In fact, by the end of the Council, there were only twelve laywomen and ten religious women present as auditors, without a vote and no right to speak unless called upon by a bishop (Abbott, 1966:500).

Even though women's voices were seldom heard at Vatican II, one statement in the document on the laity reads: "Since in our times women have an ever more active share in the whole life of society, it is very important that they participate more widely also in the various fields of the Church's apostolate" (Abbott, 1966: 500). Soon after the adjournment of the Council in 1965 many bishops and priests encouraged the laity, both men and women, to participate more actively in their dioceses and parishes; and subsequently parishioners began to see women performing such roles as Eucharistic ministers, lectors, acolytes, pastoral team associates, spiritual guides in retreats, Bible-study and prayer-group leaders, counselors, chaplains, and even administrators of priestless parishes.

The appointment of laity as pastoral administrators in priestless parishes is becoming more frequent as fewer and fewer priests are being ordained around the world (Hoge, 1987). The need for lay administrators is especially acute in rural areas and in the poorer parishes of the inner cities; and thus far, most of those appointed have been women, many of whom belong to religious communities (Gilmour, 1987). It is important to know whether a majority of lay Catholics approve of this practice, and thus whether most parishioners would welcome lay administrators in their parishes. One woman, for instance, who is a pastoral administrator in a very poor urban parish, told us that her greatest fear when she was deciding whether or not to accept the job was that many of the parishioners might leave the parish if she were appointed. Later she was relieved and overjoyed that, with only one or two exceptions, people did not leave on her account.

In addition to Vatican II changes, the new Code of Canon Law made some provisions for the expansion of women's roles in the Church. While still excluding women from the ordained ministry, the new Code opened the following positions to women: diocesan chancellors, auditors, assessors, defenders of the marriage bond, promoters of the faith, judges on diocesan courts, members of diocesan synods and financial administrative councils, and professors and board members of seminaries (Wallace, 1988:27).

If we could visit chancery offices across the United States we would discover that women are still predominantly visible as secretaries. However, we would also find that there are a few dioceses where women are now serving in positions which were formerly reserved to the clergy, such as superintendents of schools, professors in diocesan seminaries, directors of Catholic Charities, editors of diocesan newspapers, judges and other marriage-tribunal officials, and even chancellors of dioceses. These important changes were made possible by Vatican II and the revisions in the Code of Canon Law.

Women were also invisible in such roles as student or faculty member in Catholic seminaries prior to Vatican II, for women were not admitted to Catholic schools of theology for ministerial preparation until after the Vatican Council ended in 1965. At the present time, approximately one-fourth of the students enrolled in Roman Catholic theological schools in the United States are women (Baumgaertner, 1986:87-89), and a few female professors have been appointed as well.

Why is this increase in women's presence as students and professors in Catholic seminaries so significant? Until recently, only those priests who went to college *before* entering the seminary had the experience of a college education which included women as students and/or teachers. But most future priests studied for their college degrees in seminaries or schools of theology. Thus many of the priests today, as well as most of the bishops, have had little experience beyond high school in working with women as intellectual equals. The only women visible in pre-

Vatican II seminaries were the "good Sisters" who did the cooking and laundering, and the occasional cleaning women.

The Laity's Views on Women's Participation

In our national study of the laity, we asked a series of questions about lay participation. A large majority of Catholics said that the laity should have the right to participate in activities such as the following: deciding how parish income should be spent (81% agreed), giving occasional sermons at Mass (69% agreed), teaching in diocesan seminaries (68% agreed), deciding whether or not to have altar girls (66% agreed), being in charge of a parish when the priest is absent (65% agreed), selecting the priests for their parish (57% agreed), and making church policy about birth control (53% agreed).

In the early stages of our study, when we pretested our questionnaire with approximately 100 Catholics, we separated the participation questions by gender, asking first if lay *men* should have the right to participate, and then if lay *women* should have the right. We wanted to see whether Catholics would label some participation as more appropriate for men, and some as more appropriate for women. What we found was that our respondents consistently made no distinctions between men and women. They said that BOTH lay men and lay women should or should not have the right to participate in these matters.

Therefore, on the final version of our questionnaire we simply asked about laity, not specifying women or men. This is important to keep in mind as we present our data. It means that the attitudes regarding the rights of Catholic laity refer to the rights of *both* women and men.

We asked about eleven areas of church life in the question regarding the right of lay participation. Four of them are pertinent here because these are activities which have typically been "off limits" for women.

Table 6.1

In These Areas Of Church Life, Should The Catholic Laity Have The Right To Participate, Or Not? (Percents)

	Laity Should	Laity Should Not	Not Sure
Giving occasional sermons at Mass	69	26	5
Teaching in diocesan seminaries	68	23	9
Deciding whether or not to have altar girls	66	28	6
Being in charge of a parish when the priest is absent	65	27	8

They are 1) "Giving occasional sermons at Mass," 2) "Teaching in diocesan seminaries," 3) "Deciding whether or not to have altar girls," and 4) "Being in charge of a parish when the priest is absent." (See Table 6.1)

As we can see from Table 6.1, about two-thirds of American Catholics think that lay men and women should have the right to participate in giving sermons at Mass, teaching in seminaries, deciding about altar girls, and being in charge of a priestless parish. Only about one-fourth think the laity should not participate in these activities, and less than one-tenth are not sure. Table 6.2 presents the breakdowns for the key variables we have used throughout the book.

Looking first at age, we see notable differences between the under-55 age groups and those 55 and over, but even the oldest group shows a majority in favor of the laity's right to give sermons, to decide about altar girls, and to take charge of parishes in the priest's absence. Somewhat the same pattern appears among educational groups. Those with at

Table 6.2
Percentage Saying Catholic Laity Should Have The Right To Participate In Each Area of Church Life

	Giving Sermons	Teaching in seminaries	Deciding about altar girls	In Charge of parishes
All:	69	68	66	65
Age: 18-29	71	--*	72	71
30-39	75	--	78	67
40-54	79	--	68	67
55 or over	54	--	50	58
Education:				
Some High School	56	56	52	--*
High School Graduate	68	68	66	--
Some College or Vocational School	77	73	71	--
College Graduate or More	77	79	78	--
Income:				
Under $10,000	61	58	59	61
$10,000-$19,999	62	69	61	65
$20,000-$29,999	73	72	77	61
$30,000-$39,999	77	79	64	77
$40,000 and over	78	70	68	67
Importance of the Catholic Church to you personally?				
The most important part of my life	-- *	-- *	54	52
Among the most important	--	--	64	64
Quite important, but so are other areas of my life	--	--	70	69
Not terribly important, or not very important to me at all	--	--	73	73

*Breakdown with less than 12 percentage point differences are not shown.

least a high-school diploma are much more likely to opt for the laity's right of participation, but even among those who did not graduate from high school, a majority favor lay participation. Overall, the college graduates show the highest percentages on the "should" response, from 77% to 79%.

Income differences are somewhat clear on the right to give sermons and teach in seminaries; those at either extreme show notable differences, and the middle three groups are similar. However, on the laity's right to decide whether or not to have altar girls, and to administer priestless parishes, the pattern is less clear. On the altar-girl question the only important differences are between those whose income is under $10,000 and those in the $20,000 to $30,000 level; and on the question about administering parishes the most pro-participation are in the income categories above $30,000. Thus, as with other findings, the higher income groups have higher percentages saying the laity should have the right to participate.

Finally, we look at the patterns with respect to the church importance question. Here the principal differences are between those who say the Church is the most important part of their lives and all the other groups. On both the altar girl question and on the issue of lay men and women administering parishes, about two-thirds of those with the middle and low scores on church importance say the laity should have the right to participate. However, even the high scorers on church importance show a majority in favor.

Not shown in Table 6.2 are breakdowns by gender and by Mass attendance, because men and women were similar in their attitudes towards the right of the laity to participate, as were those who attended Mass often and those who attended less often, seldom, or never. All of the breakdowns showed a majority agreeing that the laity, that is, *both* men and women, should participate in giving occasional sermons at Mass, in teaching in diocesan seminaries, in deciding whether or not to have altar girls, and in being in charge of a parish when the priest is absent.

Post-Vatican II Changes

Although Vatican II encouraged female participation, a limitation to their empowerment was contained in the formal declaration from the Vatican issued on February 3, 1977, which rejected ordination for women. With respect to the text in Galatians 3:28 about nondiscrimination betweeen Jew and Greek, slave and free, male and female, the Vatican declaration argued:

> Nevertheless, the incarnation of the Word took place according to the male sex: this is indeed a question of fact and this fact, while not implying an alleged natural superiority of man over woman, cannot be dissociated from the economy of salvation: it is, indeed, in harmony with the entirety of God's plan as God himself has revealed it, and of which the mystery of the covenant is the nucleus (1977, p. 522, cited in Neal 1979, p. 237).

Many Catholic women viewed this statement as sexist because it was an affirmation of their inferior status, whereas others accepted it in the spirit of obedience to a higher authority. Eleven years later, on April 12, 1988, the American bishops issued the first draft of a pastoral response to women's concerns. The document condemns sexism as a sin, and recognizes that "sexist attitudes have also colored church teaching and practice over the centuries and still in our day." Quoting an earlier statement by two American bishops, the document states:

> Sexism, directly opposed to Christian humanism and feminism, is the erroneous belief or conviction or attitude that one sex, female or male, is superior to the other in the very order of creation or by the very nature of things. When anyone believes that men are inherently superior to women, or that women are inherently superior to men, then he or she is guilty of sexism. Sexism is a moral and social evil (U. S. Bishops, 1988:763).

The pastoral document, elaborating on sexist attitudes, states that some men, including clerics, assume they have the right to dominate women. Such attitudes when found in the Church, the document warns, "only serve to reinforce society's depersonalization of women." A dramatic example of clerical sexism came from Catholic women who reported to the bishop's committee that priest-counselors told them to "offer up to God" the abuse of their husbands (p.763).

Some of the document's recommendations which address the issue of seminary training state (p. 782):

> We also recommend that all programs for the formation of candidates for the diaconate and priesthood should emphasize the importance of clergy being able to work cooperatively on equal terms with women and without abrasive competition. The sin of sexism should be recognized for what it is, and attitudes tending toward it or an incapacity to deal with women as equals should be considered as negative indications for fitness for ordination. . . . We further recommend that women be included on the faculties and staffs of institutions responsible for the formation and education of candidates for the diaconate and priesthood.

Although the pastoral document also recommends that the question of women being ordained as deacons be investigated, this falls short of the expectations of numerous Catholic women and men who argue that the basic impediment to female empowerment in the Church is ordination to the priesthood. As Dolan (1985:439) describes it, the need to reexamine the nature of priesthood is "the most explosive issue" in contemporary Catholic life, and the issue of women priests is especially divisive, "as many theologians argue for the ordination of women, while the hierarchy, taking their cue from the Pope, remain strongly opposed to it."

Another post-Vatican II event strongly affecting women was the encyclical of Pope Paul VI, *Humanae Vitae*, which we discussed in Chapters 1 and 3. What are the Catholic laity of the late 1980s thinking about the Church's teachings about birth control, and about women's ordination? We probed such views in the 1987 survey, and we will turn to these findings now.

Church Commitment and Teachings on Women's Issues

Our 1987 survey showed that women have a high degree of commitment to the Church. When we examined all of the items on our questionnaire, we found that gender made a difference on two very important questions: the importance of the Church to you personally, and Mass attendance. 58% of the women said that the Church was the most important or among the most important parts of their lives, compared to 39% of the men. While a majority of women (52%) said that they attended Mass at least weekly, only about a third (36%) of the men replied in this way. Also, when we asked about leaving the Catholic Church, 61% of the women said they would never leave, compared to 50% of the men (see Chapter 2, Table 2.2). It is no wonder, then, that lay women are so active in the parish, because, by these measures, the Church is much more a part of their identity than it is for lay men. If we could hear the voices of *all* Catholic women, those who oppose as well as those who favor change in the Church, they would be saying in one loud chorus, "This is OUR church."

In our national survey we asked lay Catholics how some of the Church's teachings or policies affected their commitment to the Catholic Church. We mentioned eight items in all, but only three are pertinent to our discussion of women's issues. These are 1) "The Church's teaching that artificial contraception is morally wrong," 2) "The Church's teaching that abortion is morally wrong," and 3) "The policy of ordaining men, but not women, to the priesthood." After mentioning each of the teachings or policies, we asked if it strengthened their commitment to the Catholic Church, weakened it, or had no effect one way or the other. The results are shown in Table 6.3.

As we can see in Table 6.3, none of the response categories drew a majority on any of these three questions. With regard to the Church's teaching that artificial contraception is morally wrong, the laity were almost as likely to say it had no effect on their commitment to the Catholic Church (43%) as to say that it weakened their commitment (35%).

Table 6.3

Have These Teachings Or Policies Strengthened Your Commitment To The Catholic Church, Weakened It, Or Had No Effect One Way Or The Other? (Percents)

	Strengthened	Weakened	No Effect
Teaching that artificial contraception is morally wrong	13	35	43
Teaching that abortion is morally wrong	45	19	32
Policy of ordaining men but not women to the priesthood	20	25	47

Respondents feel very differently about abortion, compared to the other two issues. Only 13% of the laity said that the teaching on contraception strengthened their commitment to the Church, in contrast to a near majority (45%) who said that the Church's teaching on abortion strengthened their commitment. Only 19% said the abortion teaching weakened their commitment, and about a third said it had no effect. When we examined all of the responses on our commitment question, we found that the highest percentage responding "strengthened" was on the item regarding the abortion teaching (45%).

How do our findings on abortion compare to earlier research? The Gallup Poll has asked the following question a number of times since 1973 (Gallup and Castelli,1987:93-94): "The U.S. Supreme Court has ruled that a woman may go to a doctor to end pregnancy at any time during the first three months. Do you favor or oppose this ruling?" The percentage of Catholics who favored this ruling increased from 32% in 1974 to 47% in 1983, and the percentage of those opposed decreased from 61% in 1974 to 48% in 1983. Although this is not the same question we asked, it could be argued that those who said the Church's teaching on abortion strengthened their commitment to the Church would also oppose the Supreme Court ruling. The percentage we found upholding the Church's teaching (45%) is close to the 48% opposing the Supreme Court ruling in 1983.

With regard to the ordination of women, a near majority (47%) of the laity in our study said that the Church's policy of ordaining men but not women had no effect on their commitment, a fourth of the respondents said it weakened their commitment, and only a fifth said the policy strengthened it. Gallup polls have shown increasing support for ordaining women priests, from 29% in 1974 to 36% in 1977 to the most recent poll in 1985, when Catholics were found to be evenly divided on this issue, with 47% agreeing and 47% disagreeing (Gallup and Castelli, 1987:56). Because our question concerns church commitment rather than simply a support of the teaching, it is difficult to compare these findings; indeed we cannot even speculate about the percent supporting women priests among those 47% who replied "no effect." However, our data indicate greater support than opposition to women priests, since they show that a larger percentage of the laity said the church policy of not ordaining women weakened their commitment than those who said it strengthened it.

Overall, we can see in Table 6.3 that a near majority of our laity replied that the contraception teaching and the ordination policy had no effect on their commitment. On the other hand, when asked about the abortion teaching, a near majority replied that their commitment to the Church was strengthened by it. The laity's attitudes on these teachings and policies strongly affecting women—contraception, female ordination, and abortion—do not seem to be consistent.

We decided to look more closely at the data regarding the weakening of church commitment because these are especially pertinent to our analysis of the limited empowerment of women. Since women were excluded from the formulation of the teachings and policies on these issues, we would expect that Catholics concerned about women's limited empowerment would experience a lessening of their church commitment

Figure 6.1

Percent Saying The Teaching That Contraception Is Morally Wrong Weakened Their Commitment To The Catholic Church

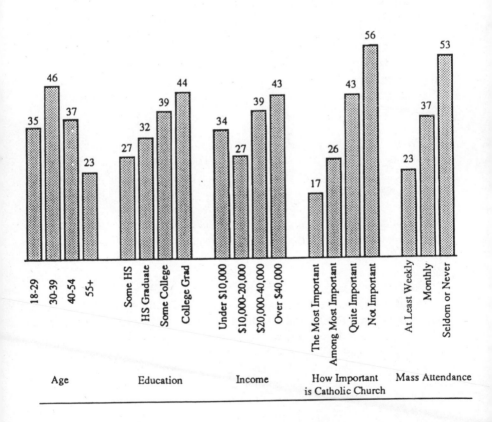

in the light of church leaders' actions. Table 6.4 shows some breakdowns on these issues.

Looking first at the teaching on contraception, we see that age, education, and income have the expected relationship. For younger, more
highly educated, and more affluent Catholics, the teaching is more likely
to weaken commitment. So also for those who seldom attend Mass and
for whom the Church is not very important. Note that a near majority of
laity in their 30s (46%) said that the contraception teaching weakened
their commitment. This is not a surprising finding, since women in this
age group are nearing the end of their child-bearing years and are
making choices about family size (see Figure 6.1).

The same pattern holds for ordination, but with less intensity. This
makes sense, for Catholics who are younger, more highly educated, and
not the most committed to the Church are more likely to be bothered by
the contraception teaching which affects them personally. The policy on
ordination, on the other hand, is less concrete for them, less a part of
their daily lives.

With regard to the abortion teaching, Table 6.4 shows similar patterns
regarding age, education and income. The subjective and behavioral
measures of commitment (importance of Church and Mass attendance)
come through as expected. However, the lower percentages indicate that
on the issue of abortion the laity are much more responsive to the teachings of the Vatican. This certainly reflects the great effort made by
church leaders to make the issue of abortion a top priority (Gallup and
Castelli, 1987:91).

Not shown here are comparisons by gender, because men and women
were similar in their attitudes about these issues. One-third of both men
and women said that the contraception teaching weakened their commitment and one-fifth said the abortion teaching weakened their commitment. But on the policy of not ordaining women, 30% of the men and
22% of the women said it weakened their commitment. This difference
is not surprising, because women attend Mass more often than men and

Table 6.4
Percentage Saying The Teaching Or Policy Weakened Their Commitment To The Catholic Church

	Contraception Morally Wrong	Abortion Wrong	Not Ordaining Women
All	35	19	25
Age: 18-29	35	-- *	27
30-39	46	--	35
40-54	37	--	22
55 or over	23	--	18
Education:			
Some High School	27	-- *	19
High School Graduate	32	--	23
Some College or Vocational	39	--	28
College Graduate or More	44	--	34
Income:			
Under $10,000	34	20	25
$10,000-$19,999	27	17	21
$20,000-$29,999	42	16	22
$30,000-$39,999	36	18	33
$40,000 and over	43	29	34
Importance of the Catholic Church to you personally?			
The most important part of my life	17	8	12
Among the most important parts	26	12	19
Quite important, but so are other areas of my life	43	23	31
Not terribly important, or not very important to me at all	56	39	40
Frequency of Mass Attendance:			
At least weekly	23	11	19
Almost every week, monthly	37	18	29
Seldom or never	53	33	34

*Breakdowns with less than 12 percentage point difference are not shown.

are, therefore, more likely to be satisfied with the situation as it is: a male priesthood. When we examined our data on gender, age, and education we found that women in their 30s and women college graduates responded more like men on the ordination issue. 29% of women who are in their 30s and 30% of women who were college graduates said the policy of not ordaining women weakened their commitment. This makes sense, because, as we have seen throughout the chapters in this book, Catholics with a college education and those in their 30s are more change-oriented.

To summarize these three issues, the teaching on contraception shows the greatest negative impact on church commitment among younger Catholics (especially those in their 30s), college graduates, the more affluent, and those who were already less committed to the Church in general. The ordination policy also tends to weaken rather than strengthen commitment, but to a lesser degree than the contraception teaching. Only on the abortion teaching is the laity's commitment strengthened, and this finding may reflect the success of the "Seamless Garment" approach, the U.S. bishops' strategy of addressing abortion in the context of issues concerned with human life at all stages, a priority of the bishops in the 1980s.

Discussion and Conclusion

The aim of this chapter was to describe and explain the changing position of women in the Catholic Church. As we pointed out earlier, the first draft of the United States Bishops' pastoral document on women's concerns issued in April of 1988 attempted to address Theresa Kane's 1979 challenge regarding women's status in the Church. The bishops' committee discovered some impediments to women's increased participation at the parish level. The document states: "Qualified women would like to share more fully in the governing and fiscal bodies of dioceses and parishes but, as they reported, the support which they need to facilitate advancement and access to such leadership positions is not forthcoming" (p. 775). What we have learned by our national study is that a majority of the laity will be strongly supportive if the recommendations of this pastoral document regarding increased participation of women in the Church are implemented.

The laity opposed to greater empowerment of women will probably not be a silent minority, however. A quote from one of the women who participated in the discussions preliminary to the drafting of the U.S. bishops' pastoral on women (p. 766) is illustrative: "I believe that reaffirmation of *Humanae Vitae* is one of the important issues for the bishops to address. . . . Once the ban on artificial birth control was challenged, it was . . . easy to take the next step and (question) the Church's position on premarital sex, abortion, divorce and remarriage."

Although the woman quoted above is content to have church leaders continue to define church teachings, we have found, on the contrary, that most Catholics want greater lay participation. On the other hand, the bishops did not have to strain to hear the strong voices of alienated women, especially on the issue of birth control. As they translated it:

The most frequently mentioned source of . . . alienation was the issue of birth control. Women brought forward experiences of great personal pain and suffering related to this issue. When they spoke of their pain, they spoke of marriages that broke up; of years spent living in guilt outside the Church; of praying for physical problems serious enough to warrant . . . (a) hysterectomy; of years of life wasted in frustration and bitterness that might have been years of married love; of finding peace of mind only after childbearing years were over or husbands had died; of going to priests for comfort and receiving instead more misery and harsh recrimination, of seeing mothers, sisters, daughters and granddaughters living the same pain (p. 766).

As we have seen in this chapter, the issue with the greatest negative impact on Church commitment was the Church's teaching on contraception. Our findings underline the need to reevaluate the Church's position on this issue.

In responding to the pastoral document, some traditional women criticized the work of the bishops' committee. One woman (Hitchcock, 1988:4) said, "Modeled on the consciousness-raising sessions of the women's liberation movement of the mid-1960s, which encouraged women to 'tell their stories' of alienation and oppression, the bishops' 'listening sessions' on which their pastoral response was based did not reveal the genuine concerns and problems of most Catholic women and their families."

Our data disconfirm this woman's assertion. In this chapter we have shown that a majority of Catholics think that Catholic lay men *and* women should have the right to participate in giving sermons at Mass, teaching in diocesan seminaries, deciding whether or not to have altar girls, and being in charge of priestless parishes. In other chapters we have presented data which show that a majority of Catholics also think that lay men and women should have the right to participate in deciding how the parish income should be spent, in selecting the priests for their parish, in making church policy about divorce, and in making church policy about birth control. We should point out that the the bishops' pastoral draft does not present the results of a national survey, and that a survey like ours is needed to supplement such a document so that we can see whether individual attitudes reflect the attitudes of the Catholic population as a whole.

What can findings of our national survey tell us about the future? In the responses to our question about the Church's teaching that artificial contraception is morally wrong, a majority of those who seldom or never attend Mass and those who said the Church was not important to them said it weakened their commitment. This was not an unexpected finding, for these groups are the most disaffected. But we also found that there were three other groups who, by a near majority, also agreed that their commitment was weakened: 1) Catholics in their 30s, 2) college graduates, and 3) the most affluent. All three of these groups were more likely to question the Church's teachings on artificial contraception.

Why is this so? We should expect college graduates, who are generally the most affluent, to question the Church's teachings. The formation of an autonomous individual is, after all, a primary goal of higher education, and social researchers have found that more highly educated groups are consistently more change-oriented. With respect to the age factor, we suggest that women in their 30s are more deeply affected by the contraception issue; more of them are likely to be currently involved in making decisions about whether or not to have children, since they are nearing the end of their child-bearing period and probably intend to limit the size of their families. Also, women's greater participation in the labor force and their participation in the contemporary women's movement have contributed to a questioning stance, rather than a position of "blind obedience."

In addition, as Sullivan (1987:10-11) pointed out, the people born between 1948 and 1957, those who are now between 30 and 39, are the people from the baby boom, the largest single group of our population, and she describes them as "trend-setters." In commenting on the findings from our study, Sullivan describes the Catholics in their 30s thus:

> I find them a very distinctive group. One way in which they are distinctive is that they're the ones who are most likely to say that Vatican II strengthened their commitment to the Church. And they are the ones most likely to say that *Humanae Vitae* weakened it. But they are still, I think, extraordinarily loyal to the Church. Vatican II came at a critical time. It came at the time of the adolescent conversion experience for them. And it was during Vatican II that they made the decision whether, as adults, they were going to be Catholic or not.

Limited empowerment is the subtitle of this chapter, and we have illustrated those limits for the female half of the Church. Are there signs that these limits are expanding or contracting? In spite of the reports given to them by alienated women, the bishops stood by *Humanae Vitae*, recommended yet another study regarding ordination and a thorough investigation on the question of admitting women to diaconal office. On the other hand, they also recommended women's participation in all liturgical ministries not requiring ordination, including lectors, acolytes, preachers, and retreat masters, and they also encouraged the hiring of women as professors in seminaries. Interestingly enough, the bishops themselves address the issue of women's limited empowerment when they state (p. 781):

> In the light of Jesus' teaching and practice, we reject actions by which women have been undervalued, subordinated, made objects of suspicion, condemnation, condescension or simply ignored. Clericalism in pastoral ministry often expresses patronizing attitudes that need to be eliminated. Men and women must work together as responsible, capable persons for the common good of church and society. We intend, therefore, to ensure that women are empowered to take part in positions of authority and leadership in church life in a wide range of situations and ministries.

Given the present shortage of priests, and the findings from the 1987 national survey showing the laity's views on increased participation, we should not be surprised about the increasing numbers of women who are being appointed as administrators of priestless parishes, as diocesan chancellors, as canon lawyers and as seminary professors throughout the United States (Wallace, 1988). These appointments represent an expanded empowerment of women in the Church, and the experiences of these women in their daily lives demonstrate that they can and are doing the work of priests. What we can predict from our study is that a majority of the laity will be supportive of a greater empowerment of women in the Church. This prediction will, of course, be discouraging for those who oppose change in the Church, but it should be an encouraging message for others.

References

Abbott, Walter M. 1966. *The Documents of Vatican II*. New York: America.

Baumgaertner, William L. (ed.). 1986. *Fact Book on Theological Education:1985-86.* Vandalia, OH: Association of Theological Schools.

Dolan, Jay P. 1985. *The American Catholic Experience: A History from Colonial Times to the Present.* New York: Doubleday.

Gallup, George, Jr. and Jim Castelli. 1987. *The American Catholic People: Their Beliefs, Practices, and Values.* New York: Doubleday.

Gilmour, Peter. 1986. *The Emerging Pastor: Non-Ordained Catholic Pastors.* Kansas City, MO: Sheed & Ward.

Greeley, Andrew M. 1985. *American Catholics Since the Council: An Unauthorized Report.* Chicago: Thomas More.

Hitchcock, Helen Hull. 1988. "Pastoral is 'Essentially Incoherent'." *National Catholic Reporter* 24 (April 29): 4.

Hoge, Dean R. 1987. *The Future of Catholic Leadership: Responses to the Priest Shortage.* Kansas City MO: Sheed & Ward.

John Paul II. 1983. *Code of Canon Law.* Washington, D.C.: Canon Law Society.

Morris, Joan. 1973. *The Lady Was a Bishop.* New York: Macmillan.

Neal, Marie Augusta. 1979. "Women in Religious Symbolism and Organization." *Sociological Inquiry* 49:218-50.

Sullivan, Teresa A. 1987. Interview in *National Catholic Reporter* 23 (September 11):10-23.

U.S. Bishops. 1988. "Partners in the Mystery of Redemption: A Pastoral Response to Women's Concerns for Church and Society." *Origins* 17 (April 21):757-88.

Wallace, Ruth A. 1975. "Bringing Women In: Marginality in the Churches." *Sociological Analysis* 36:291-303.

Wallace, Ruth A. 1988. "Catholic Women and the Creation of a New Social Reality." *Gender and Society* 2:24-38.

Weakland, Rembert. 1987. Interview in *Origins* (October 1): 262.

7.

Catholic Contributions: Why Aren't They Higher?

All institutions cost money to operate, and institutions with good monetary support can better achieve their goals. Churches are no exception. So it is natural that Catholic church leaders have long been concerned about financial contributions. This chapter looks at Catholics' contributions to their parishes, and it attempts to explain a key finding of recent studies—that Catholics contribute less to their churches than do Protestants or Jews.

Old-timers never tire of telling stories about Catholic fund-raising in the old days. Until the 1920s, the most common methods were pew rents and plate collections. Families were assessed a certain amount for a pew, depending on their income. But that did not produce enough revenue. Each parish also engaged in a round of money-raising events such as card parties, dinners, raffles, entertainments, and the ubiquitous game of Bingo. A highpoint of each year was the annual festival or bazaar, which in many places raised half of the income for the year (Dolan, 1985).

In the 1920s Sunday envelopes were widely introduced. The purpose was to encourage regular weekly contributions of an amount pledged in an annual pledge drive. The envelopes were greeted with passive resis-

146

tance, since now the priests could keep track of contributions by each family and the information might possibly be made public. But in time the laity became accustomed to the envelopes, and the new method did help raise more funds.

By all accounts, lay people had strong feelings about financial accountability and decision-making. Why did the priests have so much power to gather and disburse funds without even reporting the amounts to the laity? How could everyone be sure the money was honestly spent for the good of the parish? Why did the priests always have to preach about money? (One parish history during the 1920s indicated that 25 percent of the Sunday sermons each year were financial appeals.) Whose parish was it anyway, and why didn't the priests and bishops pay their own bills? A sense of ownership and responsibility for the parish did not develop well in those years, when there was no consultation with parishioners.

While research on church contributions has been done repeatedly in the Protestant community, little has been done in the Catholic Church.[1] The best Catholic studies, to our knowledge, have been those carried out by Greeley and his associates. In 1976, Greeley, McCready, and Mc-Court analyzed nationwide surveys of Catholics done in 1963 and 1974, asking about money spent on Catholic school tuition and about contributions to the Church. Then in 1987 Greeley and McManus published a review of all existing survey data on Catholic giving. In the 1963 survey, Catholics reported average family contributions of $164 to the Church (2.1% of income), and in 1974 they reported an average of $180 (1.3% of income). A 1975 nationwide survey by Survey Research Center, University of Michigan, found a figure of 1.6% for Catholics. A Gallup poll in 1978 found that 22% of American Catholics said they gave 5% or more of their income to the Church; the corresponding figure for Protestants was 36% (Gallup, 1984). Then in a Gallup survey and a

---

1. The Protestant research extends back several decades. See Douglass and Brunner (1935); Johnson and Cornell (1972); Hoge and Carroll (1978); Carrol, Johnson, and Marty (1979); Hoge and Polk (1980); and Hartley (1984).

Yankelovich survey in 1982 and 1984, the Catholic figure on contributions dropped to 1.1% of family income, while the Protestant figure remained at the higher level of 2.2% (Greeley and McManus, 1987:14).

Other evidence confirms that Catholic contributions are lower than Protestant contributions, even if we take into account the differences in family income in various denominations. Hoge reviewed the research and found that in 1984 the average Lutheran member in the U.S. contributed $205 to the Church, while the average Catholic member contributed about $125. The comparison between Lutherans and Catholics is instructive, since the Lutherans are culturally more similar to Catholics than are most other Protestant denominations, and Lutheran family income is almost exactly the same as for Catholics (see Hoge, 1987:51). A 1987 study looked at 201 parishes in four denominations and found that the average contribution per Catholic family was $276, while the equivalent Lutheran figure was $653. This study did not have a true random sample of parishes, thus the figures have no claim to representativeness. But the parishes were selected using uniform criteria, so any bias would be similar in both denominations; and the *relative* size of the two figures is fairly reliable (Hoge, Carroll, and Scheets, 1988).

Why do Catholic contributions lag behind Protestant levels? Greeley and McManus tried in 1987 to find out. They started by testing five hypotheses. First, are Catholics inherently less generous than Protestants? By looking at the amount of money Catholics and Protestants contributed to other charities in 1984, Greeley and McManus concluded that the Catholic-Protestant differences were small; giving to nonreligious charities was roughly the same in the two groups. Also, Catholics did not differ from Protestants on attitudes toward caring for needy persons and toward government welfare programs.

Second, do Catholics earn less money than Protestants? No. All recent surveys (as noted above) agree that they have slightly *higher* average family income. For example in the 1984 Yankelovich survey, the Catholic average family income was $27,500, and the Protestant average was $26,400.

Third, do Catholics have larger families, hence less money to spare? Yes, Catholic families are larger, but when this factor is controlled statistically (for example, by comparing Catholic and Protestant contributions just in 5-person families), Protestant-Catholic differences in contributions remained.

Fourth, do Catholics spend more on school tuition, and therefore have less discretionary income left over? Greeley and McManus controlled for school tuition costs, and still the Protestant-Catholic differences remained, indicating that the tuition factor is not important.

Fifth, are Catholics less committed to their religion than Protestants? No, the differences in several measures were small. In nationwide surveys Catholics were always found to go to church even more than Protestants (for example, in 1984, 57% of Catholics and 45% of Protestants said they go almost every week), and Catholics were similar to Protestants when they estimated how important religion is in their lives (in 1984, 54% of Catholics and 59% of Protestants said it was a very important influence).

These five hypotheses did not uncover any important explanation for the lower Catholic contribution level, but several other findings from the data were revealing. The greatest Protestant-Catholic differences in giving occurred among those persons with higher income and higher levels of education. Also, the greatest differences were among the people who considered religion important and who attended church regularly. That is, Protestants who considered religion important in their lives and attended church regularly gave much more than Catholics with similar views, whereas Protestants who were less devout and observant were similar to their Catholic counterparts. For some reason strong commitment inspired higher levels of giving among Protestants than similarly strong commitment inspired among Catholics—while weak commitment was associated with low giving in all the churches.

By re-analyzing the older 1963 and 1974 studies, Greeley was able to test some additional hypotheses. In those eleven years, contributions dropped most among the socially liberal Catholics (that is, those putting most emphasis on the Church's social mission) and among those who rejected the Church's teaching in opposition to birth control in the 1968 encyclical *Humanae Vitae*. Greeley came to the conclusion that the loss of church moral authority after the publication of the encyclical was the single most important influence causing the dropoff in contributions. The reforms of Vatican II were not a cause of the dropoff, since in 1974 the Catholics who supported the Vatican II reforms contributed relatively *more*, not less.

Greeley's hypothesis about the loss of church moral authority remains a plausible explanation for the decline in contributions. A full examination requires further testing with additional data. We have no reason to doubt the analysis which Greeley has done, and we believe future research should build on it. The 1987 survey has some new information which is useful, and we turn to it now.

Annual Contributions in 1987

The survey asked, "How much money would you say your household contributes to the Catholic Church each year, not counting school tuition?" This wording was taken directly from the N.O.R.C. survey in 1974, possibly the best study of Catholic contributions to date. In 1987, 28% either refused or said they didn't know, while 72% gave the interviewer an amount. Is the 28% refusal rate an important source of bias?

We were able to identify the categories of people who disproportionately reported or did not report their contributions. The main predictors of reporting them were amount of education and amount of family income. Respondents with college degrees or more education had an 83% response rate, compared with 58% for those with less than a high-school education. And respondents having incomes over $30,000 had an 84% response rate, versus 59% for those with incomes under $10,000.

Other variables were weaker predictors of willingness to tell an interviewer one's contribution to the Church. Age had a small predictive power, in that older people refused a bit more often (of those over 55, only 62% responded). Men responded more often than women (76%, compared with 68% of the women). People who said the Catholic Church was not very important to them tended to respond more often; at the one extreme (the Church being very unimportant) the responding rate was 81%, while at the other extreme it was 68%. Frequency of Mass attendance, however, was not associated with the rate of response.

A final bit of evidence comes from various questions about what it takes to be a good Catholic and whether laity should have the right to be involved in church decision-making. On most of these questions, the respondents who said "don't know" or "unsure" were the same ones who had a lower response rate concerning financial contributions; apparently they were unsure about their contributions too.

In sum, the least educated, the lowest in income, the most committed to the Church, and the most unsure in their attitudes about church decision-making were the people under-represented in the 1987 data on church contributions. This is a mixed picture, but the most probable conclusion is that low contributors are slightly under-represented, so the resulting national average reported is too high. How much did Catholics contribute?

The amount varied widely, with low figures most common, as shown in Figure 7.1. Forty-eight percent reported contributions between 0 and $200 per year; 20% reported $201 to $400; 15% reported $401 to $600; and the other 17% reported over $600. A few reported very large contributions; five said they gave $10,000, and ten others said they gave between $5000 and $7000 (out of 1045 total in weighted data).

Figure 7.1 shows that the bulk of American Catholics contribute less than $600 per household per year. Because of a few large donors, the mean (arithmetic average) was $502, while the median (the middle case when all are arranged in order) was $250. To exemplify the effect of the

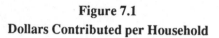

Figure 7.1
Dollars Contributed per Household

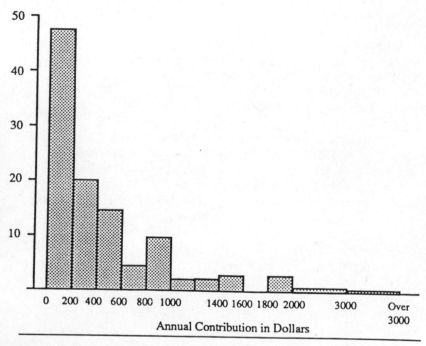

few big givers on these statistics: if the fifteen people who reported contributions of $5000 or more had exaggerated by 25%, that is, if those who said they gave $10,000 actually had given only $8000, and so on, the mean of the contributions would have been reduced to $482.

We believe there is a slight upward bias in the data. The interesting point is that the estimate from the 1987 survey is a good bit higher than in other recent surveys. In the high-quality Yankelovich survey of 1984 the average contribution per Catholic household was $320. And our 1987 estimate was $502. Why the discrepancy?

We looked into the data collection procedures in the 1984 and 1987 surveys for possible clues. We found that in 1984 12% of the sample (a sample of all adult Americans) refused to answer the question about charitable contributions or were unable to come up with a figure. In 1987 the equivalent figure in the Catholic sample was 28%. Herein lies some of the problem, since in 1987 we lacked information for a larger number of respondents (28% versus 12%). It is also important that of the persons who did respond in 1984, 28% said they had made no religious contributions in the previous year. In 1987 the figure was 9%. So the 1984 sample includes a larger percentage of non-givers than in 1987. What if we look only at the people who gave to their Church in the previous year and told the interviewer the amount? Then in 1984 the mean for Catholics was approximately $449, and in 1987 it was $554—a difference of only $105. Our best estimate of the mean contribution for all Catholic families in 1987 is therefore $420 to $450.

There is a related discrepancy in the percentage of family income contributed to the Church. Greeley and McManus calculated that in 1984, Catholics gave 1.2% of their income to the Church. In the 1987 data the figure was roughly 1.9%.[2] What is the reality? Based on the calculations above, our estimate of the reality in 1987 is about 1.5% to 1.7%. (Nevertheless we use the 1.9% figure for the further analysis shown below.)

Influence on Contributions

We have found that the average reported contribution in 1987 was $502, though we suspect that in reality it was between $420 and $450. Some families contributed more, others less. Why?

---

2. To find this percentage we divided the amount of contribution by household income before taxes. The question on income had eight responses, the highest of which was "$40,000 and over," and 19% of all respondents chose it. After several trials we assigned $55,000 to this category for calculation purposes; this produced the most plausible outcome in view of other research. Then the estimated mean family income wass $28,600. Yankelovich (1986) found a mean of $27,500 for American Catholics in 1984.

The most likely factor is the amount of family income; the more money a family has, the more it can contribute to the Church. All research demonstrates the importance of this factor. It is such an obvious determinant that in our data analysis we looked both at total dollars contributed and also at the *percent* of family income contributed. In search-

Table 7.1

Effect Of Background And Religious Commitment on Contributions

	Dollars Contributed	Percent of Family Income
Total	$500	1.9 %
Family Income Before Taxes:		
Under $10,000	240	3.2
$10,000-$20,000	340	2.4
$20,000-$30,000	380	1.5
$30,000-$40,000	730	2.2
Over $40,000	730	1.3
Age: 18-29	330	1.4
30-39	530	1.6
40-54	600	1.8
55 and over	590	3.1
Education:		
Some high school or less	300	2.3
High school diploma	410	1.6
Some college	550	2.0
College degree or more	770	2.2
Frequency of Mass Attendance:		
At least once a week	770	3.0
Almost weekly or monthly	390	1.5
Seldom or never	170	0.7
Importance of the Catholic Church:		
The most important part of my life	700	3.5
Among the most important parts	700	2.3
Quite important to me	380	1.4
Not terribly or very important	180	0.9

NOTE: Dollars contributed are rounded off to the nearest ten dollars.

ing for the explanations of high or low contributions we first looked at background information (including church commitment), then at the person's attitudes about the institutional church today.

Table 7.1 depicts the background and commitment variables most associated with level of giving. Near the top of the table is the breakdown by total family income. As suspected, families with more income contribute more to the Church. But the same is not true for *percentage* of income contributed; there it is the opposite, with the lower-income families contributing a higher percentage of the funds they have available. This is consistent with Greeley's earlier finding that the weak point in Catholic contributions is the higher-income portion of the American Catholic community.

The rest of the table shows the strongest background influences in the 1987 data. The age breakdown shows that older persons give more, both in total dollars and also in percent of income. More highly educated persons give more dollars, but not a higher percent of their income.

The last two variables in the table have the strongest relationships--frequency of Mass attendance and the importance of the Catholic Church to the respondent. Catholics who attend Mass regularly and tell interviewers that the Church is very important to them tend to give much more money. One could argue that these three measures—contributions, Mass attendance, and importance of the Church—are different measures of assessing church commitment, and that what we need to analyze is *church commitment* in general, not just contributions seen alone. Contributions, that is, depend very heavily on the person's commitment to the Church.

What is the effect of specific attitudes about the Church? Greeley hypothesized that specific areas of alienation—not total alienation—were decisive in shutting Catholics' pocketbooks. Is this the case? If so, what are they? Table 7.2 depicts the seven attitude measures having the strongest relationship to 1987 contributions. First, at the top are five parts from a series of questions asking if particular church teachings or

Table 7.2

Effect Of Attitudes About The Church On Contributions

	Dollars Contributed	Percent Family Income
Have the following strengthened your commitment to the Catholic Church, weakened it, or had no effect one way or the other?		
The Church's teaching that artificial contraception is wrong.		
Strengthened	$760	3.4%
No Effect	480	1.9
Weakened	400	1.3
The Vatican's punishment of theologians who dissent from official teachings on matters of sexuality.		
Strengthened	830	3.2
No effect	430	1.5
Weakened	440	1.6
The Church's teaching that abortion is morally wrong.		
Strengthened	600	2.5
No effect	510	1.8
Weakened	310	1.0
Recent statements by American bishops on national issues such as the nuclear arms race and the U.S. economy.		
Strengthened	720	2.8
No effect	400	1.5
Weakened	480	1.6
The Church's policy of giving preference to the poor in Latin America.		
Strengthened	630	2.6
No effect	430	1.5
Weakened	380	1.4

(Continued)

	Dollars Contributed	Percent Family Income

Who should have the final say about what is right or wrong? The church leaders—the pope and bishops; individuals taking church teachings into account and deciding for themselves; or individuals and leaders working together?

A Catholic practicing contraceptive birth control.		
Leaders	910	4.0
Both	540	2.4
Individuals	420	1.4

A Catholic advocating free choice regarding abortion.		
Leaders	770	3.1
Both	470	1.9
Individuals	370	1.3

NOTE: Contributions are rounded off to the nearest ten dollars. "Don't know" responses are not shown.

policies had strengthened the respondent's commitment to the Church, weakened it, or had no effect one way or the other. In the table they are arranged in order from the strongest to the weakest in their impact on contributions. The top three all have to do with sexuality—the Church's teachings on artificial contraception, the Vatican's punishment of theologians dissenting from teachings on sexuality, and the Church's teachings on abortion. This finding supports Greeley's conclusion that alienation of laity in the realm of sexuality is the single greatest obstacle of giving to the Church. In every case the respondents who felt that the church teachings had weakened their commitment to the Church also said they gave less money.

The next two influences are a bit weaker. They are on disparate topics, yet they have the same pattern, in that people happy with the Church give more, and those alienated from the Church give less. But these topics—statements by American bishops on nuclear war and the

U.S. economy, and the preference to the poor in Latin America—do not have the same impact as the sexuality issues.

At the bottom of the table are two of the items discussed earlier regarding where final moral authority should reside. These two had the strongest association (of the items on final moral authority) with the percentage of income contributed. In both cases the people who believe church leaders should be the final moral authority contributed by far the most money. Those endorsing individual conscience as final moral authority contributed the least, while those desiring the participation of "both" were between. As in the top of the table, contraception is the single most consequential issue.

Possibly the relationships in Table 7.2 appear to be stronger than they are in reality, since the impact of earlier background factors has not been controlled. Background factors may account for both the church attitudes and contributions, and until their impact is estimated the analyst cannot get a reliable picture of the impact of church attitudes alone. What appears on the surface to be an impact from church attitudes may really be (indirectly) caused by some of the background factors. To check this, we carried out regression analyis, which gives the impact of the attitude variables while all other influences are controlled. We found that controlling for background factors made no difference, and the actual predictive power of the attitudes is roughly as shown in the table.[3]

From Table 7.2 we learn that anything strengthening one's commitment to the Church will encourage contributions. The topics having the greatest effect on overall church commitment appear to be those in the

---

3. We regressed dollars contributed and percent of income contributed on the variables in Tables 7.1 and 7.2—with the exception of the question on importance of the Church (last item in 7.1) which was conceptually too close to dollars contributed to be useful. When we studied percent of income, it was also a part of the percentage figure. All the regressions were weak. On dollars contributed, the background variables (Table 7.1) accounted for 7.5% of the variance, and the attitude variables (Table 7.2) added another 4.7%. On percent contributed, the background variables accounted for 4.1% on the attitude variables added 9.2%. Taken alone, the attitude variables accounted for 4.4% of dollars contributed and 10.5% of percent contributed.

area of sex—contraception and abortion. Also, the Catholics who defend church authority on the sex issues contribute more money to the Church than other Catholics. Why is this? Do traditional Catholics with long-term, strong church commitment also defend institutional church authority on moral questions? Or have those Catholics alienated from the institutional Church, due to sex issues, cut down on their contributions? Whatever the truth may be, it is associated with generalized church commitment more than specific topics or issues. Each household's level of contribution is a resultant of diverse influences encouraging or discouraging giving that are pulling in different directions; thus, specific issues have some influence, but are not very decisive. More important is the overall commitment to the parish by household members.

At the bottom of Table 7.2 we saw that the people most strongly defending church authority on moral questions are those who contribute the most, while those desiring the participation of both church leaders and individuals contribute less. Also, we saw in Chapter 4 that many Catholics would favor some change in church processes of moral decision-making to allow more participation by laity. Now the question arises: Would contributions rise, or fall, if the processes did change in this way? We could predict that defenders of church authority would find the change offensive and would cut down their contributions, while those desiring more participation would in turn contribute more. Would the net result be a gain or a loss in contributions? It is an important question, but with available data we do not know.

Conclusions

The 1987 survey allowed us to test the impact of various attitudes on church contributions. Most had only a modest impact. For example, questions about democracy and lay participation at the local level did not affect levels of contributions. We also found that the amount of Catholic education a person had received was not crucial, nor was the region in which he or she is living. What was important was overall church commitment, which in turn is influenced by acceptance of church moral teachings and acceptance of ultimate church moral authority. Moral issues in the area of sexuality are the most important, especially contraception and abortion. What Catholics believe on these two questions greatly determines their level of giving.

Greeley found, when comparing Protestant and Catholic giving, that the big difference was in the high-education and high-income groups. High-income Protestants contribute much more than high-income Catholics. Apparently there is a feeling of alienation from the institutional Church felt by high-income Catholics, and from our 1987 data it would appear to be mainly in the realm of sex teachings. By contrast, low-income and less-educated Catholics don't feel such a problem. But when high-income people begin to feel alienated, one can expect a strong effect on contributions to the Church, and apparently this has happened.

We began this chapter by looking at Greeley and McManus's comparison of Protestant and Catholic giving to the Church. The level of Catholic giving is lower, and the question is why. Greeley and McManus said that Protestants are no more religious or devout, on the average, than Catholics, so the difference must reside somewhere in factors related to the institutional Church. They thought that alienation from Catholic moral teachings was a principal reason. The 1987 survey had new data to help clarify the situation, and from our analysis we conclude that in general Greeley and McManus are right; lay feelings about Catholic moral teachings are crucial. Contraception and abortion seem to be the single issues having the most impact on laity. But these issues are not alone, and we believe the most accurate analysis would look at overall faith in the Church more than at single specific moral issues. We also discovered, in analyzing the 1987 survey, that American Catholics desire more participation in the process of formulating moral teachings. This has an important implication for stewardship, in that more participatory processes in the future would probably strengthen average church commitment among laity.

Catholic stewardship experts and fund-raising consultants have come to conclusions not much different from ours. They have found that parishes with the greatest increases in contributions in recent years are those who have begun issuing detailed giving and expenditure reports to the lay members. Laity appreciate greater openness in parish finances and greater involvement of lay leaders in decisions about parish money (see Unsworth, 1987). So there appears to be hope for improved financial support for American Catholic parishes as they move in the direction of greater lay participation, more open financial accountability, and an enhanced sense of ownership of the parish by all the People of God.

References

Carroll, Jackson W., Douglas J. Johnson, and Martin E. Marty. 1979. *Religion in America: 1950 to the Present.* New York: Harper and Row.

Dolan, Jay P. 1985. *The American Catholic Experience.* Garden City, NY: Doubleday.

Douglass, H. Paul, and Edmund de S. Brunner. 1935. *The Protestant Church as a Social Institution.* New York: Harper and Row.

Gallup Organization. 1984. *Religion in America.* Gallup Report No. 222. Princeton, NJ: Gallup Organization.

Greeley, Andrew M., William C. McCready, and Kathleen McCourt. 1976. *Catholic Schools in a Declining Church.* Kansas City: Sheed and Ward.

Greeley, Andrew M., and William McManus. 1987. *Catholic Contributions: Sociology and Policy.* Chicago: Thomas More Press.

Hartley, Loyde H. 1984. *Understanding Church Finances: The Economics of the Local Church.* New York: Pilgrim Press.

Hoge, Dean R. 1987. *The Future of Catholic Leadership: Responses to the Priest Shortage.* Kansas City: Sheed and Ward.

Hoge, Dean R., and Jackson W. Carroll. 1978. "Determinants of Commitment and Participation in Suburban Protestant Churches." *Journal for the Scientific Study of Religion* 17:107-17.

Hoge, Dean R., Jackson W. Carroll, and Francis K. Scheets. 1988. *Patterns of Parish Leadership: Cost and Effectiveness in Four Denominations.* Kansas City: Sheed and Ward.

Hoge, Dean R., and David T. Polk. 1980. "A Test of Theories of Protestant Church Participation and Commitment." *Review of Religious Research* 21:315-29.

Johnson, Douglas W., and George W. Cornell. 1972. *Punctured Preconceptions: What North American Christians Think About the Church.* New York: Friendship Press.

Unsworth, Tim. 1987. "Parish Finances: Are Catholics Reluctant to Pay Their Own Way?" *U.S. Catholic* 52 (September):32-8.

Yankelovich, Skelly, and White, Inc. 1986. *The Charitable Behavior of Americans: A National Survey.* New York: The Independent Sector.

8.

The Pastoral Letters on Peace and the Economy: A New Approach to Church Teachings

In 1983, the American Catholic bishops published a pastoral letter expressing their opposition to the continuing arms buildup and the use of nuclear weapons. The letter outlined "universal principles" and called for "immediate bilateral agreements to halt the testing, production and deployment of new nuclear-weapons systems." It condemned first use of nuclear weapons by any nation; said that the bishops were "highly skeptical" that "a 'limited' nuclear war could remain limited"; and insisted that any "nuclear response to either conventional or nuclear attack" that goes "beyond legitimate defense" is "morally unjustified." Finally, it argued that storing nuclear weapons was tolerable only as an interim step in the direction of disarmament.

Three years later, the bishops issued another pastoral letter, this time questioning some of the nation's economic policies and calling for more "economic justice." The economic pastoral used biblical and theological concepts such as "creation," "convenant," and "community" to develop a moral vision which says that all economic decisions "must be judged in light of what they do for the poor, what they do to the poor, and what they enable the poor to do for themselves." The bishops use this vision to analyze four issues: employment, poverty, food and agriculture, and the global economy. Among other things, the letter asserted "current levels of unemployment are intolerable and they impose on us a moral obligation to work for policies that will reduce joblessness"; that "the distribution of income and wealth in the United States is so inequitable that it violates (the) minimum standard of distributive justice"; that there is a need to reexamine federal farm policies and tax laws which benefit large farms more than small ones; and that we must "eliminate 'the scandal of the shocking inequality between the rich and the poor' in a world divided ever more sharply between them."

The two letters—which are extensions of traditional Catholic social teachings dating back to Pope Leo XIII's encyclical *Rerum Novarum* in 1891—were meant to be "teaching tools" in Catholic parishes and schools. But the bishops also wanted to reach a much wider audience and frame public debate which might lead to changes in America's economic and political policies.

Two things made these letters controversial: the unusually democratic way in which they were prepared (over 100 experts were interviewed for each letter, the media were invited to listen to the bishops' discussion of the drafts, and lay people were invited to send in written responses to early drafts), and the fact that these relatively "liberal" letters were published during a very "conservative" period in American history.

The letters received extraordinary amounts of media coverage. All the major news magazines devoted considerable space to early and final drafts of both letters. *Time* magazine (April 11, 1983: 82) called the peace pastoral "a sweeping critique of U.S. nuclear-deterrence strategy at the very time when President Reagan is caught up in a tense international struggle over the issue." *Newsweek* (May 16, 1983: 26) said it "is by far the most ambitious and daring political statement the bishops have ever produced."

U.S. News and World Report (November 26, 1984: 59) said the economic pastoral "urges vast changes in economic policy—most in direct conflict with the Reagan philosophy." *Newsweek* (November 19, 1984: 97) called the letter "a thoroughgoing, thought-provoking repudiation of the Reagan administration's supply-side economics, and a call to reexamine economic priorities in light of the Church's 'preferential option for the poor'."

Catholic commentators also saw the letters as controversial. In the most noteworthy case, former Treasury Secretary William Simon, social commentator Michael Novak, and other members of the Lay Commission of Catholic Social Thought and the U.S. Economy published their own letter on the economy two weeks prior to the first draft of the bishops' letter. Theirs was a vigorous defense of America's capitalist economy—which they felt the bishops were going to criticize too severely—and a plea that the bishops not place too much emphasis on reforms which require governmental intervention in the private sector.

Given the importance of these letters for Catholics and non- Catholics alike, and the controversies surrounding both of them, we wondered what American Catholics thought about them. How many Catholics have heard or read about the pastoral letters (four years after the publication of the peace pastoral and more than a year after the economic pastoral was issued)? Which Catholic laity are most, and least, aware of the letters? Which Catholics tend to agree or disagree with the letters' controversial recommendations? What impact do these letters have on Catholics' commitment to the Church? Finally, what impact are they likely to have on authority relationships between the laity and the hierarchy, and on the democratization of the Church in general? Our findings are summarized in the next section of this chapter and are followed by a discussion of their implications for clergy and lay leaders.

Awareness of the Pastoral Letters

One of our questions asked: "In 1983, the American bishops issued a pastoral letter about the arms race and nuclear weapons. Have you heard or read about this letter?" Another asked: "In 1986, the American bishops issued a pastoral letter calling for changes in the U.S. economy. Have you heard or read about this letter?" The responses are in Table 8.1.

Table 8.1
Awareness of the Pastoral Letters (percent)

	Peace Pastoral	Economy Pastoral
Have heard of or read it	29	25
Have not heard of or read it	67	71
Not sure	5	4

In light of all the media attention given to the publications of these two letters, we were surprised to find that the majority of American Catholics were not aware of either one. Sixty-seven percent had not heard of the peace pastoral, and 71 percent had not heard of the economic pastoral. An even more recent poll (*Our Sunday Visitor,* May 1, 1988: 7) indicates that 85 percent of the Catholics in the diocese of Gary, Indiana, do not know what is in the economic pastoral. Clearly, the pastoral letters are not yet a part of the Catholic laity's consciousness.

The data in Table 8.2 indicate that those who have heard of the letters, so far at least, are some of the most accessible groups of Catholic laity: highly educated, affluent, active Catholics. People who have gone beyond high school, have considerable Catholic schooling, are in white-collar occupations, and have high family incomes are most likely to know about both letters—though in most cases, not even a majority of these Catholics have heard of them. (See Figure 8.1 for a summary.)

The bishops have had the most difficulty reaching the groups which the Church has always had the hardest time reaching: less educated,

Table 8.2

Awareness of the Pastoral Letters by Categories (percent)

	Have Heard of:	
	Peace Pastoral	Economic Pastoral
Race		
Whites	31	25
Blacks	17	39
Ethnicity		
Irish	36	32
German	33	31
French	28	32
Italian	27	17
Polish	22	19
Hispanic	16	15
Other	26	21
Occupation		
Business	32	38
Manager/Executive	42	37
Professional	51	32
Clerical/Sales	26	17
Service	18	18
Skilled	31	23
Semi-skilled	16	19
Laborers	7	16

(continued)

	Have Heard of:	
	Peace Pastoral	Economic Pastoral
Amount of education		
More than High School	42	33
High School Graduate	25	21
Less than High School	10	16
Catholic education		
Three levels	63	44
Two levels	34	29
One level	29	26
None	24	21
Income		
$40,000 or more	45	36
$20,000 to $40,000	29	25
Less than $20,000	22	23
Region		
Southwest	15	22
West Central	44	39
Southeast	18	10
Middle Atlantic	31	28
New England	32	20
East Central	24	24
Pacific	31	22
Rockies	27	20
Age		
55 or more	29	27
30-54	35	26
29 and under	19	20
Mass attendance		
Daily/Weekly	37	31
Almost Weekly	26	22
Seldom/Never	17	17

Figure 8.1

Percent of Catholics Who Have Heard of Each Pastoral Letter

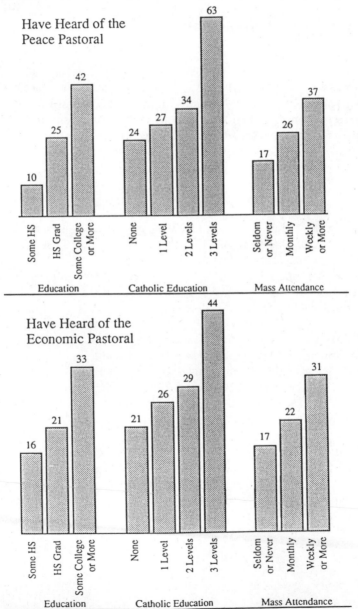

lower-income Catholics who are not active in the Church. As a rule, fewer than one-fifth of the people in these "marginalized" groups know anything about the letters. Clearly, the Church needs to do an awful lot more than it has so far to inform *all* the laity, *especially* groups which it finds hardest to reach.

The only variable on which there is a difference between the two letters was race: Whites are more likely to have heard of the peace pastoral; Blacks are more aware of the economic pastoral. There are no significant differences between men and women, or between married and single Catholics. Total amount of education has somewhat more impact than years of Catholic schooling does.

Opinions About The Letters

Once the letters were published, people wondered how Catholics would react to their contents. Church leaders, all the TV networks, and all the newsmagazines asked how many—and which—Catholics would agree or disagree with them. To find out, we asked Catholics who *were* aware of the letters whether they agreed or disagreed with their contents. Our results are summarized in Table 8.3.

A majority of those Catholics who had heard of the letters agreed with their contents. There seems to be somewhat more agreement with the economic pastoral (71 percent) than with the peace pastoral (57 percent). However, there is a sizable minority of Catholics who either disagree with the contents of these letters or are not sure what to think (43 percent for the peace pastoral and 29 percent for the economic pastoral).

While the patterns in Table 8.2 concerning *awareness* are quite similar for both letters, they are quite different regarding *opinions* of the letters' contents (see Table 8.4). Groups which respond most favorably to one letter are not necessarily the most enthusiastic about the other. So we will treat the two letters separately in this section of our analysis.

Table 8.3
Overall Agreement/Disagreement with the Pastoral Letters
(percent of those who had heard about the letters)

	Peace Pastoral	Economic Pastoral
Agree	57	71
Disagree	29	21
Don't know	14	8

We examined four sets of factors which might affect Catholics' attitudes about the two pastorals: socio-demographic factors (such as age, education, occupation, and income), religious factors (such as frequency of Mass attendance and financial contributions), conceptions of what it takes to be a "good Catholic" (for example, whether one could be a good Catholic without going to Mass every Sunday, without obeying the Church's position on birth control, or without donating to help the poor), and attitudes about decision-making processes at three levels: the parish, the diocese, and the Vatican.

Peace Pastoral

Religious factors seem to have the most impact on Catholics' attitudes about the peace pastoral (see Table 8.4). Catholics who attend Mass almost weekly and those who donate $500 or more to the Church also tend to approve of this letter. Less active Catholics are more inclined to disagree with what the bishops had to say.

Catholics' attitudes about decision-making in the Church also are related to their attitudes about the peace pastoral. Catholics who feel there ought to be more democratic decision-making are more inclined to agree with the letter than Catholics who are apt to accept current decision-making processes.

Overall, socio-demographic factors have some, relatively modest, impact. Whites (especially Irish and German Catholics) blue-collar (especially semi-skilled) workers, Catholics with moderate levels of education, and Catholics who live in the Rocky Mountain region were most likely to approve of the letter's contents.

Somewhat surprisingly, Catholics' conceptions of what it takes to be a "good Catholic" are relatively inconsequential. Though we expected that "liberal" Catholics who are willing to dissent from traditional church conceptions of what it takes to be a good Catholic would be most inclined to embrace the peace pastoral, there are no appreciable differences between "liberals" and "conservatives" who feel one must stick to traditional expectations to be a good Catholic. There are significant differences on only one item: liberals who feel one can be a good Catholic and still practice birth control are more likely to agree with the peace pastoral than those who take a more conservative view on the birth-control issue.

Economic Pastoral

The pattern is quite different regarding the economic pastoral: socio-demographic factors are the most important influences; conceptions of being a good Catholic have only limited effects; religious factors and attitudes about decision-making are largely irrelevant.

Marginalized Catholics (e.g., Blacks, Catholics with less education, blue-collar jobs, and relatively low incomes) are more inclined to agree with the economic pastoral than Catholics who are in higher socio-economic strata. These data are consistent with another recent study by Tamney, Burton, and Johnson (1987). Social characteristics have more impact on Catholics' attitudes about the economic pastoral than their religious orientations do.

Conceptions of being a good Catholic have far fewer effects than we expected, and the limited effects they do have are not in the direction we expected. In the two items which did achieve statistical significance, Catholics who feel that one ought to adhere to traditional standards regarding Mass attendance and birth control are more inclined to agree with the economic pastoral than liberal Catholics who say adherence to these traditional standards are not necessary.

Religious commitment has virtually no effect: those who are most loyal to the Church, attend Mass most often, and give the most money to the Church are no more likely to agree (or disagree) with the letter than less active Catholics. The same is true for attitudes about decision-making processes: they also have no bearing on Catholics' views of the economic pastoral.

To summarize, the peace pastoral tends to be supported by religious Catholics who yearn for a more democratic Church; their socio-demographic characteristics and conceptions of being a good Catholic are largely irrelevant. The economic pastoral is supported most by marginalized Catholics who are not much different from other Catholics except perhaps in their tendency to be somewhat more traditional on the birth-control issue and on the importance of going to Mass.

Impact of Letters on Commitment

Finally, we asked Catholics what effect these pastoral letters have had on their loyalty to the Church (see Table 8.5). As one might expect, based on the overall lack of awareness shown earlier in Table 8.1, the letters seem to have had rather limited impact: 43 percent of Catholics say the pastorals have had no effect on their commitment to the Church. But the letters' net effect has been more positive than negative: 27 percent say the letters have strengthened their commitment; 16 percent say they have weakened it; and 14 percent say they don't know what the impact has been.

Given this variation in the impact of the letters, we wondered if those who agreed with the letters were any more likely to say the letters in-

Table 8.4

Opinions about the Pastoral Letters by Categories (percent)

	Agree with:	
	Peace Pastoral	Economic Pastoral
Socio-demographic factors:		
Gender		
Men	65	74
Women	69	81
Race		
Whites	57	69
Blacks	36	100
Ethnicity		
Hispanic	51	70
Irish	73	85
Germans	70	76
Italians	59	74
Poles	65	90
French	44	52
Other	67	77
Occupation		
Business	67	57
Manager/Executive	70	75
Professional	56	75
Clerical/Sales	73	81
Service	20	79
Skilled	73	68
Semi-skilled	83	100
Laborers	--	75

(continued)

	Agree with:	
	Peace Pastoral	Economic Pastoral
Amount of Education		
High School or More	65	30
High School Graduate	70	60
Less than High School	52	91
Catholic education		
Three Levels	66	77
Two Levels	72	85
One Level	61	75
None	70	71
Income		
$40,000 or more	60	66
$20,000 to $40,000	69	77
Less than $20,000	58	89
Region		
Southwest	43	56
West Central	74	82
Southeast	64	73
Middle Atlantic	70	86
New England	52	64
East Central	67	70
Pacific	69	94
Rockies	80	93
Marital status		
Married	66	67
Single	68	53
Age		
55 and over	53	69
30-54	56	69
29 and under	62	75

(continued)

	Agree with:	
	Peace Pastoral	Economic Pastoral
Religious factors:		
Likelihood of leaving the Church		
Most unlikely (score 1)	57	70
Most likely (score 2-7)	57	72
Mass attendance		
At least weekly	56	72
Almost Weekly	62	71
Seldom/Never	52	67
Contributions		
$500 a year or more	66	70
$250 to $500	58	70
$250 or less	51	70
Concept of being a "good Catholic":		
Liturgical practices		
Can you be a "good Catholic" without—		
going to church every Sunday?		
Yes	58	66
No	55	81
going to private confession at least once a year?		
Yes	54	67
No	62	74
Personal morality		
obeying the Church's teaching on birth control?		
Yes	62	67
No	45	80
obeying the Church's teaching on abortion?		
Yes	60	71
No	55	71

(continued)

	Agree with:	
	Peace Pastoral	Economic Pastoral
Economic behavior		
Donating time or money to help the poor		
Yes	50	70
No	61	70
Contributing to Peter's Pence		
Yes	57	71
No	49	74
Decision-making in the Church		
Should there be more democratic decision-making at the:		
Parish level		
Yes	61	71
No	43	73
Diocesan level		
Yes	61	72
No	47	67
Vatican level		
Yes	59	71
No	52	71

creased their commitment to the Church than those who disagreed with their contents. Or, has the publication of these pastoral letters strengthened or weakened Catholics' commitment, regardless of their opinions about the letters' contents?

The data in Table 8.5 show that Catholics who tend to agree with the contents of the two letters also say that the publication of the letters has strengthened their commitment to the Church, while those who disagree with their contents are much more inclined to say that the letters have weakened their attachment to the Church.

Table 8.5

Impact of Pastoral Letters Overall and by Agreement/ Disagreement (percent)

	Strengthened	Weakened	No Effect	Don't Know
Recent pastoral statements by American bishops on national issues such as the nuclear arms race and the U.S. economy	27	16	43	14
Peace Pastoral				
Agree	50	12	35	3
Disagree	19	42	39	--
Economic Pastoral				
Agree	48	17	26	9
Disagree	18	47	30	5

Thus, the letters have neither a uniformly positive, nor a uniformly negative, impact on the nation's Catholics. They solidify the commitments of those who agree with them, but foster some alienation among those who disagree.

Implications

These data concerning some of the bishops' most important and controversial activities during the 1980s have several implications for understanding the Church and Catholic Americans.

The secular media and most Catholic publications like the idea of bishops' writing pastoral letters which address matters in the economic and political arenas. Certainly, there have been some dissenting voices, but—by and large—the feeling (also expressed in our findings) is that it is all right for Catholic bishops to write such letters. For every person who objects, there seem to be twice as many who think it is an important, and perhaps even essential, pastoral and prophetic function.

There also seems to be considerable support for the open process the bishops used in writing both letters. Commentators, both outside and inside the Church, express the view that such an open process is good for the Church. We concur, believing that the democratic way in which the letters were written represents an important step in the direction of sharing responsibility with the laity. It is a signal to the laity that their input is appreciated and that they can play an important role in shaping church teachings in areas such as the economy and nuclear arms.

Thus, lay people (and others outside the Church) are receptive to the idea of bishops using an open, democratic process to develop pastoral letters on important subjects such as peace and economic justice. We would assume that they also would respond positively to the use of such a participatory process in the formation of pastoral letters on topics such as the role of women in the Church, birth control, and abortion.

Our data also tell us that the letters have reached the same resourceful people who are reached by most conventional channels of church communication: those with the most (Catholic) education, the best jobs, and the highest incomes. These people don't always agree with the letters' contents, but at least the letters have entered their consciousness.

The pastoral letters—even in the highly publicized way these two letters were produced—have not produced widespread awareness of their contents. Two-thirds of Catholic Americans have not heard of the peace pastoral four years after it was published, and 71 percent have not heard of the economic pastoral (at a time when economic inequalities are a growing concern). The letters do not seem to be having the widespread impact that some writers (e.g., Castelli, 1987) seem to think.

Our data suggest the bishops are having difficulty reaching the relatively marginalized groups which the Church traditionally has had the hardest time reaching: less educated, blue-collar, lower-income, minority Catholics. If the Church wants to increase members' knowledge of the letters and the issues they address, it also must have an educational plan which reaches the poorest and most inactive Catholics as well as those who are higher in status and more active in the Church.

What about those Catholics who are reached? What about the ones who do hear about the letters? Should they agree with the letters' contents? Will they?

The bishops' view is that Catholics are expected to agree with their most general interpretations of scripture and church teachings, and should give serious consideration to their more specific recommendations, though—in all good faith—the laity may disagree with some or all of these recommendations. Thus, the bishops hope for some consensus on basic theological principles but expect—and make room for—considerable 'dissent on more concrete issues where some laity and clergy alike may have good reasons for alternative views. In our view, this posture is a significant advance over the more rigid expectations of the pre-Vatican II period and—if applied to issues of personal morality as well as economic justice and nuclear arms—can be a healthy and invigorating force in the post-Vatican II era.

The evidence in this chapter suggests that Catholics respond quite differently to the two letters. Those who are most involved in the Church and want it to be more democratic tend to agree with the peace pastoral, regardless of their socio-demographic characteristics and their conceptions of what it takes to be a good Catholic. On the other hand, it is socio-demographic characteristics—not religious commitment or belief—which explain Catholics' views of the economic pastoral: marginalized Catholics (regardless of their religious beliefs and practices) tend to favor the letter, while more established Catholics (also regardless of the nature and extent of their faith) are more likely to oppose it.

These findings suggest that when pastoral letters address survival issues of concern to all Catholics regardless of other self-interests, Catholics are most likely to respond in terms of values (e.g., national security), and those who are loyal to the Church and want to participate in its decisions the most will be most likely to respond favorably. These sorts of letters are likely to promote involvement and solidarity in the Church.

However, when pastoral letters deal with issues which are more closely related to the laity's and the clergy's self-interests, these interests will have an important effect on the way Catholics respond. Pastoral letters which address interest-oriented issues (e.g., economic justice, the role of women in the Church) will foster open disagreements among Catholics who may be equally faithful but have conflicting social, economic, and political interests. Thus, for example, if the final draft of the latest pastoral on women speaks to womens' interests as clearly as the economic pastoral spoke to the interests of the poor, women will tend to support it and many men—both clergy and laity—may be troubled by it. If it does not speak to womens' interests as forcefully, it will tend to reinforce male dominance and further alienate women in the Church.

Finally, this chapter gives us some insight into the "seamless garment" debate. Whether we are clergy or laity, our worldviews are shaped by church teachings, our self-interests, and other normative forces (such as our ethnic heritages and our parents). Because our interests and sociocultural backgrounds are frequently so different, we tend to interpret church teachings differently. Thus, there always will be differences of opinion among clergy and among lay people. Theologically, the seamless garment may be a desirable goal, but sociologically it is difficult—if not impossible—to achieve.

References

Castelli, Jim. 1987. "A Tale of Two Cultures." *Notre Dame Magazine*, May.

Newsweek, 1983. "The New Push For an Arms Deal." May 16: 26.

Newsweek, 1984. "God as Social Democrat." November 19: 97.

Our Sunday Visitor, 1988. "Recent Survey Responses Yield 'Interesting Results'." May 1: 7.

Tamney, Joseph B., Ronald Burton, and Stephen Johnson. 1987. "Christianity, Social Class, and the Catholic Bishops' Economic Policy," paper presented at annual meeting of the American Sociological Association, Chicago, August.

Time, 1983. "The Bishops Stand Firm." April 11: 82.

U.S. News and World Report. 1984. "U.S. Bishops vs Reaganomics: A Growing Furor." November 26: 59.

9.

Summary and Conclusion

"I think all these changes started when they admitted there was no such person as St. Christopher. If they knew that, why did it take them so long to admit it?

"And things really got out of hand when they said eating meat on Friday was no longer a mortal sin. Since I was a kid, I was brought up to believe that eating meat on Friday was a sin. Now, it's not a sin. Maybe it never was a sin. So who knows what's a sin?"

These observations by a life-long Catholic suggest some of the changes are felt by American Catholic laity. First there was unquestioning obedience to church teachings, then with change came doubt about the legitimacy of authority, and then came the larger question of who knows what is right or wrong. This study has looked at several elements of the earth-shaking changes in Catholic life that have occurred in the past thirty years. Here we will summarize the main findings.

In Chapter 1, we singled out two important characteristics of American society: the importance of personal autonomy, and the responsibility of the individual for the common good. A major goal of our study was to see if these features of American society might be reflected in the current thinking and behavior of Catholic laity. For we assume that societal values and structures influence the values and structures of subgroups within it, in this case the Catholic community.

We also wanted to assess the impact of the changing characteristics of the Catholic population, that is, the way such factors as age, education, income and gender influence how the laity think and behave.

Finally, we wanted to build on the path-breaking studies already carried out by Greeley and others in the past thirty years. Thus, we decided that it was time to focus on questions of authority and decision-making, and of the laity's perception of the place of autonomy in religious matters.

In Chapter 2, we documented recent demographic changes. No longer is the Catholic Church a European-immigrant Church. Third, fourth, and now fifth generation European ethnics have moved from urban ghettoes and low-status jobs to outer city and suburban areas and to full assimilation in the American workplace. And the younger, more educated laity were found to be less committed than their forebears a generation earlier.

But this demographic change is not the whole story, since a new immigration of Hispanics is in full swing. Heavy immigration from Mexico, Puerto Rico, Cuba, and elsewhere in Latin America has caused a doubling of Hispanics in the U.S. in less than two decades. What does this mean for American Catholicism? Some experts believe Hispanics now comprise about one-third of the 52 million American Catholics. (In our survey they were less than that, at least in part for reasons having to do with the methods of data collection, as explained in Chapter 2.)

Questions are often raised about how many of the Hispanics have either converted to one of the evangelical Protestant denominations or have remained totally unchurched. Fitzpatrick (1983) reported findings from his own and other studies indicating that the proportion of Hispanics in the United States who may rightly be called Catholic may well be less than 50% of the total. For example, he noted that less than half of all marriages among Hispanics in a number of studies were Catholic marriages. Other studies have shown that 20%-30% of Hispanics belong to one or another Protestant denomination.

In religious terms, the Hispanic population may not be too dissimilar from the Italians almost a century earlier. Italians came here with high illiteracy rates, and were among the least active churchgoers of the European ethnics. Yet now into the fourth generation, Italian-Americans are pretty much in the mainstream in matters of Mass attendance (44%), contributions (46%), and subjective commitment to the Church (50%). Those findings suggest that the process of assimilation into American society may lead to a rapprochement with the Church with which the Hispanics were traditionally linked.

The "family picture" of American Catholics presented in Chapter 2 showed that the Catholic population consists of many different social and cultural groups. Catholics live in different regions of the country, although still predominating in the Northeast and Midwest areas.

Catholics in our study seem fairly committed to the Church. While less than half go to Mass weekly, more than half make it at least monthly. And two-thirds say they would never leave the Church, while a majority say the Church is the most important or among the most important parts of their lives.

In one area the level of commitment is low, and that is financial contributions to the Church. If people put their money where their values are, then the Church does not come off very well. While half of the sample earned at least $20,000 a year, two out of three contributions were less than $400.00, only 2% of gross income for the sample as a whole. Our study confirmed Greeley's findings that Catholics do not contribute according to their means.

As expected, age, education and income affect levels of commitment and participation. In general the younger and better educated were less committed than the older and less educated. However, the level of commitment increased with the number of years of formal Catholic education. Those with 16 or more years were among the most highly committed. It would appear that Catholic education does make a difference, but only eight percent of the sample had 16 years of Catholic education.

And there is little likelihood of any significant increase in the percentage of American Catholics spending 16 years in Catholic schools.

Using comparative data, we found that the level of commitment to the Church has declined from the 1950s. Then, most Catholics (75-80%) were found to be highly committed; today half or less are. But we need to take account of the changing times as we review these findings. We may well be in transition to a new definition of commitment. Clearly, going to Mass regularly remains an important sign of commitment. But even among irregular churchgoers, a majority of Catholics say they would never leave the Church and that the Church is one of the most important parts of their lives. So we are left to ponder the changes that are taking place regarding the meaning of commitment.

What are the future prospects regarding commitment to the Church?

a. The 18-29 year olds, and those in their thirties and forties, have much lower levels of commitment than those over age 55.

b. Hispanics now have the lowest commitment levels (along with low education, income, and occupation levels).

c. As Hispanics achieve upward mobility, we may expect changes in their fertility; they will have fewer children per family. There is no reason to expect them to be different from other Americans in contraception practices. Thus, there will be tension with the formal Catholic teaching authority, and probably a lowering of their level of commitment. The long-run expectation is that they will simply ignore the Church's official teachings in favor of their own experience.

Divorce will replace separation and desertion, producing further strain on Hispanics' commitment, given current church teachings. And the current high abortion rates among Hispanics is a source of still further strains. But abortion rates may be expected to drop as Hispanics gain a degree of economic and social stability.

In Chapter 3, we examined the meaning of a "good" Catholic. Our data showed that people's views have been changing. While slightly less than half of our sample went to Mass regularly, 70% said you could be a good Catholic even if you didn't. Many put little importance on matters of behavior like birth control, remarriage after divorce, getting married in Church, and private confession. Almost half also said you could be a good Catholic without believing in the infallibility of the pope. Even on the question of abortion, 39% challenged the teaching authority of the leaders by saying you could disobey the Church and still be a good Catholic. Consistent with earlier findings, age, education and income accentuated the differences. Younger, more educated, higher-income persons were the least traditional.

The ethos of American society seems to have combined with the teachings of Vatican II to encourage more personal autonomy. Traditional sacramental and liturgical practices no longer define who is a good Catholic for a majority of American Catholics. Nor are laity willing to allow hierarchy to define good Catholics by traditional standards of sexual-marital conduct.

Given the leaders' effort to make abortion the litmus test of who is a good Catholic, the fact that only 39% challenged the traditional position is evidence of continued influence. At the same time, almost half said you couldn't be a good Catholic if you did not help the poor. This response also reflected the strong efforts of Church leaders to raise the consciousness of the laity to the problems of the poor throughout the world.

It seems that the quality of contemporary Catholicism more and more is defined by whether you value human life in all its phases (Cardinal Joseph Bernardin called it a consistent life ethic) than by traditional sacramental and liturgical practices.

In Chapter 4 we examined the strength of the Church's moral authority. With the laity now in the process of redefining who is a good Catholic, it is not surprising that they are challenging church leaders' claims to a monopoly on moral authority. While Vatican II formally established the principle of the invincibility of the individual conscience, it was the issuance of the birth-control encyclical *Humanae Vitae* that seems to have stirred the consciences of individual Catholics. Greeley has demonstrated that it was the crucial turning point in the development of Catholic lay autonomy and rejection of papal authority.

In our survey, never did more than one-third of the laity acknowledge that the ultimate source of moral authority (who should decide what is morally right or wrong) should rest with the hierarchy alone. Contemporary Catholics see themselves as the proper source of moral authority, with or without the teaching of church leaders as an aid to guide them. Rejection of Vatican decrees is greatest among the young and better educated.

The rejection of the Church leaders' claims to be the arbiters of moral authority is a serious matter. In a world in search of moral authority, what might we hope for?

The 1987 survey suggests two ways in which the Church's moral authority can be strengthened. The first is to re-examine the processes of formulating moral teachings, with the aim of including as many Catholic voices as possible—clerical and lay, men and women, rich and poor—in the process. The recent example of the process the bishops used in writing the pastoral letters on nuclear war and the American economy, and the draft document on womens' issues, provides a helpful model for a new approach to moral authority in the Church. Similar processes, if encouraged at all levels from the Vatican to the local parish, would be welcome, according to our survey data.

The second is to clarify the relationship between the authority of church teachings and the informed individual's conscience. Thomas Aquinas's teaching on the importance of the well-formed individual conscience is not well understood in many places in America. The Vatican II document on religious liberty makes clear that the individual conscience has a moral claim over against church teachings! A nationwide effort to clarify the teaching and to set forth all the issues involved would be a spiritual benefit to the Catholic community, and would serve, in the long run, to increase respect for church teachings. The American Catholic laity are prepared for this kind of joint participation in decision-making. They have said they want it. Are church leaders able to hear the message?

This brings us directly to the question of democratization of the Church. Despite the claims of many church leaders to the contrary, church history is replete with evidence of democratic tendencies.

Vatican II and the special Papal Birth-Control Commission were consonant with American and western democratic processes. The issuance of *Humanae Vitae,* and other recent efforts to censure leaders like Archbishop Hunthausen and Fr. Charles Curran, and to gain control over Catholic colleges and universities—are increasingly and openly resisted. Our survey shows a majority of American Catholics wanting more democratic decision-making at local, diocesan and Vatican levels. And they want more say in matters ranging from how parish income is used, to selection of priests for the parish. The younger and better educated Catholics are most insistent on their right to participate.

The most interesting implication from our findings is that the laity want to participate in joint decision-making. They do not insist on going it alone, totally rejecting the role of the hierarchy. Nor do most of them simply want to drop out. Rather, they seem to be working toward a model of Church as voluntary association, a model consonant with the American cultural experience.

In Chapter 6 we explored the changes in the role of women in the Church in the years since Vatican II. Institutional constraints continue to impede their full empowerment. The Bishops' draft document recognized this, and recommended greater participation of women in all liturgical ministries not requiring ordination. Will the laity support this recommendation? Our data suggest that they will.

A majority of the laity in our study think that Catholic laymen and women should have the right to give sermons at Mass, to teach in diocesan seminaries, to decide about altar girls, and to take charge of priestless parishes. Based on our data we predict that women who accept an expansion of their church ministry, including such roles as administrators of priestless parishes, professors in diocesan seminaries, chancellors of dioceses, and canon lawyers, will have the support of a majority of lay Catholics.

The bishops' draft document may be seen as a small step in the right direction. From our political experience in public life, we know that it takes a long time for Congress to achieve consensus on highly controversial issues. In such cases, Congress elaborates the discussion, and does not close it off. And so we hope will the bishops on the question of the full participation of Catholic women in the life of the Church.

In Chapter 7 we asked why Catholic contributions were not higher. Members of organizations show their pleasure or displeasure with the way things are being run in several ways: they may quit an organization in protest against its policies; or they may withdraw active support, while remaining within the organization. In the latter case, withdrawing financial support is a strong measure of protest and a sign of the weakness of the organization's claim to authoritative control. Although our survey showed only a small percentage of laity are thinking of leaving the Church, our research is consistent with other studies in showing that Catholics contribute much less to their churches than do Protestants, even under identical conditions of family income-level, size of family and cost of schooling. For example, relative to Lutherans, Catholics give about half as much. The reason isn't that Catholics are less religious or more stingy. If anything they are more religious than average Protestants. But Catholic laity do not contribute in the same proportion as they did before *Humanae Vitae*, especially among the more affluent and better-educated Catholics. As a result, the Church is deprived of millions of dollars which could help to carry out its mission more effectively. Everything the Church stands for—evangelization, social witness, liberation of peoples, charity, education, healing—suffers. Simply put, the withdrawal of financial support is the most direct way the laity has to express its dissent from church leadership.

All research data indicate that greater participation by laity in church decision-making is desired by rank and file Catholics, and it would encourage financial giving at the local level. Also, greater financial reporting and accountability would encourage trust among laity that decisions are authoritative and funds are properly spent. Especially among wealthy Catholics, these measures would increase the feeling that all Catholics have a stake in the Church and its teachings, and all procedures are being properly followed. Even a modest re-thinking of church practices in these respects would seem to hold promise of increasing future contributions.

We ended our review of the 1987 study in Chapter 8 with a close look at the recent pastoral letters of the American bishops. Only a minority of American Catholics are aware of these letters, but a majority of those are supportive. If the bishops were expecting their message to reach out broadly, this has not happened. But to the extent that they encouraged participation, both from the right and left, they have been supported in their efforts, if not in all their conclusions.

Our findings revealed an important pattern of response to pastoral letters. When the contents address topics of universal concerns (e.g., world peace), people tend to react in terms of their religious orientations. Those who are most active in the Church and want more democratic decision-making tend to agree with the letters' contents; those who are less involved and do not favor more democracy in the Church tend to disagree. However, when the contents deal with issues which have more direct bearing on people's social, economic, and political self-interests (e.g., economic justice), people tend to react in terms of their interests. If the letters' recommendations are consistent with their self-interests, they will tend to agree; if not, they will tend to disagree. Thus, affluent Catholics are struggling with the pastoral on economic justice, while poor and marginalized Catholics think it a wonderful document.

Their agreement or disagreement with the letters, in turn, affects their orientation toward the Church as a whole. In general, the more Catholics agree with the pastorals, the more they identify with the Church and want to be a part of it. When they disagree, the letters have the effect of lessening their attachment to the Church.

The letters and the way they were formulated present a potential new model for the Church. It is hardly to be confused with true democratic participation, but it is a step in that direction. The most hopeful signs are: they were developed as letters, not as edicts from above; they are seen as documents for further discussion and refinement, not written in stone for the ages. Their authority rests on the degree to which people perceive them to be reasonable.

The recent draft document on women is important as a continuation of the development of more democratic processes, if it is meant as a first step. The next step will be watched with great interest. Our data show that the expansion of womens' roles has strong support from the laity, men and women.

Conclusion

The diversity among Catholics, the changing patterns of involvement, and the differing responses to the two pastoral letters call our attention to how different the post-Vatican II Church is from the pre-Vatican II Church. We have gone from a more homogeneous, European-immigrant Church in which white male dominance and obedience to church teachings were largely taken for granted to a much more heterogeneous Church in which lay people with very different values and interests are demanding the right to speak and participate in all phases of church life. While many Catholics have become alienated and left the Church, those who remain tend to be loyal and committed. Most important of all, they want to be active participants in the Church.

The pattern of leadership most likely to yield more future commitment to the Church is one that is open, tolerant, and flexible—the pattern that was demonstrated in the preparation of the pastoral letters. The process by which these letters were written contributes to a belief, even among those who disagree with their contents, that the letters are authoritative. If lay people believe their diverse views will be taken seriously and that they can have some hand in the formulation of decisions affecting their lives, their loyalty and commitment will follow.

When Pope John XXIII issued the call for Vatican II, he urged all Church members to be attentive to "the signs of the times." His words seem very prophetic for the present situation of the American Church.

References

Fitzpatrick, Joseph P., S.J. 1983. "Faith and Stability Among Hispanic Families: The Role of Religion in Cultural Transition," in William V. D'Antonio and Joan Aldous (eds.), *Families and Religions*. Beverly Hills, CA: Sage Publications.

Related Titles also Available from Sheed & Ward:

Continuing the Journey: Parishes in Transition

by Maureen Gallagher

Faced with the dwindling number of priests and a growing Catholic population, more than 40% of U.S. dioceses have begun turning to laity, vowed religious and deacons to fill parish leadership roles in the absence of resident priest-pastors. *Continuing the Journey* offers a framework and a process for approaching change, whether that change is losing a resident priest-pastor, closing a parish school, or any other major transition in a community.

The manual, written to accompany *Continuing the Journey: Parishes in Transition*, serves two purposes: to provide parish and diocesan leadership personnel with planning resources to help them design programs that will prepare parishes for pastoral change, and to suggest methods for using *Continuing the Journey* with parishes who are experiencing significant pastoral change. It is an important and much-needed resource from the Institute for Pastoral Life in Kansas City, for any group seeking to name their community loss, act upon it, and begin anew.

Participant's Book: **LL1238,** 96 pp. pb, **$5.95**
Leader's Manual: **LL1240,** 72 pp. pb, **$4.95**

The Future of Catholic Leadership: Responses to the Priest Shortage

by Dean R. Hoge

Here is the most penetrating and most reliable review of research on the priest shortage available today. Hoge describes the current situation and outlines most likely future trends. Concluding that the shortage of priest in the U.S. is an institutional problem, not a spiritual one, Hoge outlines eleven options for dealing with this problem. The options range from reconstituting parishes to reducing the demand for priestly services, redistributing existing priests, and broadening eligibility requirements for candidates for the priesthood. Richard McBrien writes: "This book should be read by every bishop, every vocation director, every member of every seminary staff, every person involved in the recruitment, formation and evaluation of ministers of every kind, and any and every individual who has ever written or lectured or just 'sounded off' on the so called vocations crisis."

LL1074, 260 pp. pb. **$12.95**